Managing Editor
Mara Ellen Guckian

Editor in Chief
Karen J. Goldfluss, M.S. Ed.

Creative Director
Sarah M. Smith

Illustrator
Clint McKnight

Cover Artist
Barb Lorseyedi

Art Coordinator
Renée Mc Elwee

Imaging
James Edward Grace
Craig Gunnell

Publisher
Mary D. Smith, M.S. Ed.

GRADE 6

Critical Thinking
Test-taking Practice for
READING

CORRELATED TO COMMON CORE STANDARDS

TCR 3919

STUDENTS WILL:
- Improve reading skills
- Gain critical-thinking skills
- Develop effective strategies to answer questions
- Become more confident test takers

Teacher Created Resources

Author
Julia McMeans, M.Ed.

CORRELATED TO COMMON CORE STANDARDS

For correlations to the Common Core State Standards, see pages 10–11. Correlations can also be found at *http://www.teachercreated.com/standards*.

Teacher Created Resources
6421 Industry Way
Westminster, CA 92683
www.teachercreated.com

ISBN: 978-1-4206-3919-3

© 2014 Teacher Created Resources
Made in U.S.A.

Teacher Created Resources

Table of Contents

Introduction

So here we are, well into the new millennium and there is still no robotic classroom assistant who grades all the papers and makes sure that no one in the back of the room is talking; still no time-travel phone booth that allows us to take our class on a trip to Independence Hall, circa 1776; and still no brain-scanning technology that instantly assesses the reading-comprehension skills of our students.

Here are the facts: Contemporary educators assess students in basically the same ways they were assessed fifty years ago—students read a passage and then they answer a question like this:

---

1. Why do you think the author is using humor to introduce the topic of test-taking to her audience?

   A. The author is trying to trick the reader into thinking this is a joke book.

   B. The author does not think test-taking is very important.

   C. The author has invented a brain-scanning device.

   D. The author is trying to use humor to introduce a stressful topic.

The answer is D. Standardized testing, whether you are the test-giver or the test-taker, is a high-stakes, stressful proposition, and for the time being, there's no getting away from all those tiny bubbles! So let's breathe deeply and try to figure out the most effective ways in which to help our students fill in all those tiny bubbles correctly!

Much has been written about test-taking strategies, most of it focused on the actual techniques that students can use to help navigate multiple-choice questions. While we acknowledge the necessity of that skill set, the focus of the books in this series is somewhat different.

This book concentrates on the requisite reading-comprehension skills that are prevalent on standardized multiple-choice tests and the ways in which we can teach students to first recognize the type of questions they are being asked, and second, to use the most effective strategies to answer specific types of reading-comprehension questions.

We believe that if students have an awareness, a kind of metacognition, about the specific skills that are evaluated and an ability to discriminate among the array of questions they are being asked, then they will become more confident and effective test-takers.

Explicit and Implicit Questions

Reading-comprehension tests primarily ask two types of overarching questions. These questions are either *explicit* or *implicit*.

Explicit Questions

Explicit questions are questions for which there is a literal, easy-to-find answer. These kinds of questions are also called "right there" questions because students can find the answer stated overtly right there in the text.

- Explicit questions often begin with the words *who*, *what*, *when*, or *where*.

- Explicit questions fall under the Bloom's Taxonomy category of *Remembering* (also known as *Knowledge*), requiring students to simply recall or locate information.

- Explicit questions are often the easiest reading-comprehension questions for students to answer.

Remember, to answer an explicit question, look for the answer written *right there* in the text. Locate it and point right to it!

Implicit Questions

Implicit questions are questions that require the reader to *read between the lines* to identify information that is often not stated literally but is implied by the text.

- Implicit questions require students to draw conclusions and to make deductions and predictions.

- Implicit questions frequently require that students make text-to-self and text-to-world connections.

- Implicit questions fall under the Bloom's Taxonomy category of *Analyzing and Evaluating*, which requires students to make judgments, compare and contrast, and distinguish between facts and opinions.

- Implicit questions are often extremely challenging for students to answer.

To answer an implicit question, use clues from the story plus your own experience. Implicit questions often begin with the word *why*.

Making Inferences and Drawing Conclusions

Drawing a conclusion based on implied information in a text is a skill that requires practice. In order to draw a reasonable conclusion and answer an inferential question, the reader must identify the unstated or implied information in a text, and then combine it with his or her own experiences and knowledge of the world (prior knowledge).

Use the "Boy in the Pond" activity on pages 7–9 to help students discriminate between implicit and explicit questions.

Explicit and Implicit Questions (cont.)

Directions: Look at the cartoon. What do you think will happen next? Is this an *explicit* or an *implicit* question? Explain.

Explicit and Implicit Questions _(cont.)

Directions: Look at the cartoon below. Is the question being asked an *explicit* or an *implicit* question? Explain.

"So tell us, Mr. Chicken, why did you cross the road?"

"Boy in the Pond" Questions

Directions: Use the illustration on the next page to help you answer these questions. Put an **I** on the short line after any *implicit* questions. Put an **E** on the short line after any *explicit* questions. Answer the questions on the longer lines.

1. Is the boy in the water? _____

   _____

2. What season is it? _____

   _____

3. Is the tree branch broken? _____

   _____

4. If the boy crawled out of the water, would the goat butt him? _____

   _____

5. Is a goat standing by the pond? _____

   _____

6. Will the branch fall on the boy's head? _____

   _____

7. How did the boy get into the water? _____

   _____

8. Why doesn't the tree have any leaves? _____

   _____

9. If it rains, will leaves will grow on the tree? _____

   _____

10. Will the boy get into trouble? _____

   _____

"Boy in the Pond" Illustration

Directions: Look at the picture. Use the illustration to answer the questions on the previous page.

"Boy in the Pond" Explanation

Below you will find a detailed explanation regarding the *implicit* or *explicit* nature of each question.

1. Is the boy in the water? _____E_____

This is an explicit question because we can see the boy in the water.

2. What season is it? _____I_____

This is an implicit question. The season (spring or summer) is hinted at by the leaves on the deciduous tree, the attire of the boy, and the recreational activity he is engaged in.

3. Is the tree branch broken? _____E_____

This is an explicit question because we can see the broken branch.

4. If the boy crawled out of the water, would the goat butt him? _____I_____

This is an implicit question. The viewer has to combine clues from the picture of the goat standing next to the pond and prior knowledge that goats often do butt people to arrive at a reasonable answer.

5. Is a goat standing by the pond? _____E_____

This is an explicit question because we can see the goat standing by the pond.

6. Will the branch fall on the boy's head? _____I_____

This is an implicit question. The picture suggests the branch will fall on the boy's head because it is broken and in the process of falling, and the boy is standing directly beneath it.

7. How did the boy get into the water? _____I_____

This is an implicit question. It is implied the boy was on the branch, it broke, and that he fell into the water.

8. Why doesn't the tree have any leaves? _____I_____

This is an implicit question because the reason is implied by picture clues. The viewer can deduce that it is spring or summer because there are leaves on nearby trees and grass growing around the pond. The tree in question has no leaves and has brittle branches. Students will have to draw on personal knowledge regarding what it means when a tree has no leaves in the growing season.

9. Will leaves grow on the tree if it rains? _____I_____

This is an implicit question. It is implied that the tree is dead. (See explanation for #8.) Therefore, no amount of rain will make a dead tree sprout leaves.

10. Will the boy get into trouble? _____I_____

This is an implicit question. We do not see the boy getting into trouble. The viewer has to use picture clues (The boy did something dangerous.) and draw on personal experience (Have I ever gotten into trouble for doing something dangerous?) to answer the question.

Common Core State Standards Correlation

Each passage and question in *Critical Thinking: Test-taking Practice for Reading (Grade 6)* meets one or more of the following Common Core State Standards© Copyright 2010. National Governors Association Center for Best Practices and Council of Chief State School Officers. All rights reserved. For more information about these standards, go to *http://www.corestandards.org/* or *http://www.teachercreated.com/ standards/*.

Reading: Literature	Page Correlations
Key Ideas and Details	
ELA.RL. 6.1 Cite textual evidence to support analysis of what the text says explicitly as well as inferences drawn from the text.	34-39, 54-57, 58-62, 78-82
ELA.RL. 6.2 Determine a theme or central idea of a text and how it is conveyed through particular details; provide a summary of the text distinct from personal opinions or judgments.	34-39, 54-57, 58-62, 78-82
ELA.RL. 6.3 Describe how a particular story's or drama's plot unfolds in a series of episodes as well as how the characters respond or change as the plot moves toward a resolution.	26-29, 54-57, 58-62
Craft and Structure	
ELA.RL. 6.4 Determine the meaning of words and phrases as they are used in a text, including figurative and connotative meanings; analyze the impact of a specific word choice on meaning and tone.	26-29, 34-39, 54-57, 78-82
ELA.RL. 6.5 Analyze how a particular sentence, chapter, scene, or stanza fits into the overall structure of a text and contributes to the development of the theme, setting, or plot.	34-39, 58-62, 78-82
ELA.RL. 6.6 Explain how an author develops the point of view of the narrator or speaker in a text.	26-29, 34-39, 54-57
Range of Reading and Level of Text Complexity	
ELA.RL. 6.10 By the end of the year, read and comprehend literature, including stories, dramas, and poems, in the grades 6–8 text complexity band proficiently, with scaffolding as needed at the high end of the range.	all passages
Reading: Informational Text	
Key Ideas and Details	
ELA.RI. 6.1 Cite textual evidence to support analysis of what the text says explicitly as well as inferences drawn from the text.	18-21, 22-25, 30-33, 40-44, 45-49, 50-53, 63-66, 67-70, 71-73, 74-77
ELA.RI. 6.2 Determine a central idea of a text and how it is conveyed through particular details; provide a summary of the text distinct from personal opinions or judgments.	18-21, 22-25, 45-49, 63-66, 67-70, 71-73, 74-77
ELA.RI. 6.3 Analyze in detail how a key individual, event, or idea is introduced, illustrated, and elaborated in a text (e.g., through examples or anecdotes).	40-44, 45-49, 63-66, 71-73, 74-77

Common Core State Standards Correlation *(cont.)*

Reading: Informational Text *(cont.)*	Page Correlations
Craft and Structure	
ELA.RI. 6.4 Determine the meaning of words and phrases as they are used in a text, including figurative, connotative, and technical meanings.	18-21, 22-25, 45-49, 63-66, 67-70, 71-73, 74-77
ELA.RI. 6.5 Analyze how a particular sentence, paragraph, chapter, or section fits into the overall structure of a text and contributes to the development of the ideas.	18-21, 30-33, 40-44
ELA.RI. 6.6 Determine the author's point of view or purpose in a text and explain how it is conveyed in the text.	50-53, 67-70
Integration of Knowledge and Ideas	
ELA.RI. 6.8 Trace and evaluate the argument and specific claims in a text, distinguishing claims that are supported by reasons and evidence from claims that are not.	50-53
Range of Reading and Level of Text Complexity	
ELA.RI. 6.10 By the end of the year, read and comprehend literary nonfiction in the grades 6–8 text complexity band proficiently, with scaffolding as needed at the high end of the range.	all passages
Language	
Knowledge of Language	
ELA.L. 6.3 Use knowledge of language and its conventions when writing, speaking, reading, or listening.	all passages
Vocabulary Acquisition and Use	
ELA.L. 6.4 Determine or clarify the meaning of unknown and multiple-meaning words and phrases based on *grade 6 reading and content,* choosing flexibly from a range of strategies.	18-21, 63-66
ELA.L. 6.5 Demonstrate understanding of figurative language, word relationships, and nuances in word meanings.	18-21, 26-29, 45-49, 54-57, 58-62
ELA.L. 6.6 Acquire and use accurately grade-appropriate general academic and domain–specific words and phrases; gather vocabulary knowledge when considering a word or phrase important to comprehension or expression.	26-29, 54-57

Process Skills

Reading-comprehension tests assess student ability in two main areas: decoding and deriving meaning. Students can expect to encounter questions that cover all of the areas outlined below on standardized assessments.

Vocabulary

Vocabulary questions on reading-comprehension tests typically ask students to identify and determine the meaning of words and word parts by employing a variety of strategies, including the following:

- Identifying synonyms, antonyms, homophones, and multiple-meaning words
- Identifying the meaning of words using prefixes and suffixes
- Using reference materials: dictionary, thesaurus, and glossary
- Using root words and word origins
- Using context clues: definition, contrast, restatement, and inference

Fiction

Reading-comprehension tests usually ask students to analyze, interpret, and/or identify the following elements of fiction:

- Characters, including their traits, feelings, beliefs, motives, and actions
- Literary devices and figurative language, including hyperbole, metaphor, analogy, anthropomorphism, alliteration, simile, personification, onomatopoeia, and idioms
- Literary elements, including plot, setting, and theme
- Poetry, including rhyme, rhythm, stanza, verse, and meter
- Genres and their characteristics, including folk and fairy tales, fiction, myths, poems, fables, fantasies, historical fiction, and chapter books

Nonfiction

Reading-comprehension tests ask students to analyze and deconstruct the following elements of nonfiction passages:

- Text structure, including compare and contrast, chronological, and cause and effect
- Author's purpose and point of view, including identifying intent, and bias
- Graphic features, including, graphs, tables, charts, etc.
- Sequence of events
- Main idea, supporting details, and extraneous information
- Details from the text that support ideas
- Distinction between fact and opinion, identifying fact or opinion
- Types of nonfiction and their characteristics, including biographies and autobiographies
- Summarizing a passage
- Paraphrasing the main idea

Remind students...
Explicit and implicit questions can be framed around many process skills. For example, there may be character-analysis questions that are both explicit and implicit.

Content References for Student Questions

Students can expect to find questions about the topics and skills listed below on reading-comprehension tests. This list may be used as a reference so that students are aware, in advance, of the types of questions they may be asked. Encourage students to review this list often. Room has been provided alongside the list for notes. Ultimately, you never want students to be surprised by the type of questions that they are being asked.

Vocabulary

Decoding and Structural Analysis
- synonyms
- antonyms
- homophones
- multiple-meaning words
- prefixes
- suffixes
- root words
- word origins

Determining Meaning
- context clues
- definition
- contrast
- restatement
- inference

Reference Materials
- dictionary
- thesaurus
- glossary

Nonfiction

Text Structure
- compare and contrast
- chronological order
- cause and effect

Author's Purpose
- point of view
- intent
- bias
- fact and opinion

Main Idea
- supporting details
- extraneous information
- paraphrasing and summarizing

Content References for Student Questions *(cont.)*

Fiction

Character Analysis

- traits
- feelings
- beliefs
- motives
- actions

Literary Devices and Figurative Language

- hyperbole
- metaphor
- analogy
- anthropomorphism
- alliteration
- simile
- personification
- onomatopoeia
- idioms

Literary Elements

- plot
    —sequence of events
    —main problem
    —conflict and resolution
- setting
- theme

Poetry

- rhyme
- rhythm
- stanza
- verse
- meter

Characteristics of Genres

- folk and fairy tales
- fiction and nonfiction
- myths
- poems
- fables
- fantasies
- historical fiction
- biographies and autobiographies
- chapter books

How This Book Is Organized

This book is organized into three tests: Test A, Test B, and Test C. Each test has 50 questions and contains a mix of the types of questions that were discussed previously. The tests are scaffolded so that the degree of assistance provided decreases with each assessment.

Test A

Test A provides students with specific and detailed guidance regarding how to approach the passages and the test questions in the form of call-out boxes along the sides of both the passage and questions. The call-out boxes are positioned beside relevant sections of text and questions. You will notice that students are asked to determine whether some of the questions are implicit or explicit. You may instruct students to indicate their responses by using either an **E** for *explicit* or an **I** for *implicit*.

Example from Test A

Directions: Read the retelling of the classic story "The Gift of the Magi." Then answer questions 41–50.

The Gift of the Magi

by

O. Henry

One dollar and eighty-seven cents. That was all. And sixty cents of it was in pennies. Pennies saved one and two at a time by bulldozing the grocer and vegetable man and the butcher until one's cheeks burned with the silent embarrassment and shame. Three times Della counted it. One dollar and eighty-seven cents. And the next day would be Christmas. There was clearly nothing left to do but flop down on the shabby little couch and howl. So Della did it. Which left Della to believe that life is made up of sobs, sniffles, and smiles, but mostly sniffles.

> At what time of the year is this story set?

45. What words best describe Della's mood at the beginning of the story?

    A. joyful and patient

    B. frustrated and sad

    C. angry and depressed

    D. envious and sad

> Consider Della's thoughts and actions.

Type of Question: _____

How This Book Is Organized *(cont.)*

Test B

Test B continues to provide call-out support, but there is less of it, and it is more general in nature.

Example from Test B

Directions: Read the passage called "The Night Sky." Then answer questions 1–10.

The Night Sky

Our moon has been the subject of many books, movies, and folklore. There is a myth that when the moon is full it can transform people into werewolves. Some tall tales claim that the moon is made of Swiss cheese because from our vantage point it looks like it is full of holes. There are still other stories that claim that there is a man who lives on the moon!

9. Most likely, why has the moon been the subject of so many songs and folklore?

   A. Many words rhyme with *moon.*

   B. Many people have been there.

   C. Everyone can see it, but most people have not been there.

   D. It is close.

   Type of Question: _____

> Implicit questions often begin with the word *why*.

Test C

Test C also provides 50 practice questions but no call-out box support. It is an opportunity for students to take a reading-comprehension assessment independently. This will give both you and your students an opportunity to see the degree to which they have internalized not only the ability to correctly identify question types, but the specific strategies they can employ to answer the questions.

How This Book Is Organized (cont.)

Answer Key

The answer key at the back of this book was designed to be another teaching and learning tool for both teachers and students. While it's important for students to know which answer is correct, it is equally useful for students to understand why the other options are incorrect. This answer key provides the correct answers to the questions, identifies the types of questions being asked, and details why the other options are incorrect.

The sample below shows the answer to the question in the example for Test B on the previous page. The answer key provides the correct answer, the specific type of question asked, and when appropriate, whether the question is *explicit* (**E**) or *implicit* (**I**). It also provides a brief explanation regarding the correct answer and information regarding why the other options are incorrect. A bubble answer sheet is also provided on page 83.

Sample Answer Key Response

9. Correct Answer: C (*Making Inferences*) **I**

The passage tells us that the moon is the subject of much myth. Myths usually grow around things that are mysterious. Our moon is a mystery to most people because most people have never traveled there. Myths are often celebrated in folktales and songs.

Incorrect Answers:

A. Many words do rhyme with *moon*, but this is not the reason there are songs and folklore about it.

B. Very few people have been to the moon.

D. The moon is relatively close, but its proximity is not the reason there are folktales and songs about it.

Test A   Name: _____

Directions: Read this passage about mummification. Then answer questions 1–10.

Ancient Egyptian Mummification

What is the first thing that pops into your head when you think about the ancient Egyptians? Is it a pyramid in the desert, some hieroglyphs etched into a block of stone, or a fearsome pharaoh? Maybe what you think about is someone or something that has been dead for thousands of years!

> Take a quick look at the questions before you read the passage.

A mummy is a dead body that has been intentionally preserved. There are lots of different ways to preserve a corpse. But nobody did it as well as the ancient Egyptians. They had special methods that they perfected over centuries. The ancient Egyptians were so good at mummification that we are still discovering their mummies today.

Religious Beliefs

There are many different religions in the world. Many of these religions believe in heaven and hell. Others believe in reincarnation. There are people who don't practice any religion. They believe that the life you live on Earth is the only life you will ever live.

Different religions also have different rituals that they practice when someone dies. Islam requires that Muslims be buried with their heads pointing toward Mecca. Mecca is the birthplace of the prophet Mohammad, who is the most important person in Islam.

> Think about how religious beliefs and rituals are connected.

Many Jewish people believe that the body belongs to God, and that it should not be defaced in any way. This is why Jews usually do not cremate or embalm their dead. *Cremate* means to burn a body after death. *Embalm* means to inject chemicals into the body to temporarily preserve it so it can be shown at a funeral.

Hindus and Buddhists usually cremate their dead. They believe that the burning of the body helps people focus on just how short and temporary life is.

You can see that different religious beliefs have a lot to do with what happens to the body at the time of death. This will help you understand why the ancient Egyptians practiced mummification.

Test A   Name: _____

Ancient Egyptian Mummification *(cont.)*

Ancient Egyptian Religion

Like all civilizations, the ancient Egyptians held strong religious beliefs. They believed that all people had a "ka" and a "ba." The *ka* is the life force. The second you are born you get a ka. The *ba* is like your conscience or personality. It is made up of the good and the bad that you do in your life. The combination of the ba and the ka is similar to the Christian idea of the soul.

> What do the *ka* and the *ba* symbolize?

The ancient Egyptians believed that after a person died, the ka could leave the body, but not the tomb. The ka would receive the offerings of food and wine that loved ones would leave at the burial place.

But what is the role of the ba? The ancient Egyptians believed that the ba left the body during the day so it could be with the gods. At night, the ba had to return. Often, you will see the ba shown as a bird flying in and out of a mummy.

> Examine the connection between the ba and the need for mummification.

Because the ba rested inside the dead body, the body itself had to be preserved. This is why ancient Egyptians practiced mummification. If nothing was done to the body after death, it would naturally decay. And if there was no body, where would the ba go to rest?

The ancient Egyptians, just like religious people today, had reasons for practicing the rituals that they did. To us, some of these may seem very unusual. But just imagine how odd a Christmas tree or the practice of yoga might seem to an ancient Egyptian!

Questions: 1–10: Select the best answer.

1. What does the word *intentionally* mean in the second paragraph?

   A. purposely

   B. accidentally

   C. deceased

   D. wrapped in linen

> Go back to the second paragraph and reread the sentence the word is in.

2. What does the prefix *em* in the word *embalm* mean?

   A. out of

   B. through the veins

   C. into

   D. between

> Think of other words you know that begin with the same prefix.

Type of Question: _____

Test A | Name: _____

Ancient Egyptian Mummification *(cont.)*

3. What determines what happens to a body at the time of death?

   A. the age of the deceased

   B. where a person dies

   C. the ba and the ka

   D. religious belief

> Look for a cause-and-effect relationship between ideas.

4. What does the author compare the ba to?

   A. the ka

   B. the life force

   C. the conscience

   D. the prophet Mohammad

> Point Right To It!

5. Why did the ancient Egyptians bury the dead with food and drink?

   A. to nourish the ka

   B. to nourish the ba

   C. to appease the gods

   D. to keep the mummy alive

> Use the headings to help locate where this information may be.

Type of Question: _____

6. Where does the ba go during the day?

   A. to the mummy

   B. to the gods

   C. to the ka

   D. to sleep beside the mummy

> Go back and reread paragraph 10 to locate the answer.

Type of Question: _____

7. Why is a bird a good representation for the ba?

   A. A bird has wings and can travel from place to place.

   B. Feathers are used during mummification.

   C. Birds are small and can fit inside a mummy.

   D. The ancient Egyptians worshipped birds.

> Think about what the ba must do each day and night.

Type of Question: _____

Test A   Name: _____

Ancient Egyptian Mummification *(cont.)*

8. Why did the ancient Egyptians mummify their dead?

    A. as an experiment to see how long the body could last

    B. so the ba would have a place to rest at night

    C. so the ka could keep the life force of the mummy intact

    D. the gods required it

> Think about the beliefs of the ancient Egyptians.

9. Which of the following could be considered the opposite of mummification?

    A. cremation

    B. entombment

    C. embalming

    D. defacing the body

> Think about what mummification was meant to do.

10. Mummification is a

    A. celebration.

    B. religious practice.

    C. political act.

    D. act of rebellion.

Type of Question: _____

Test A   Name: _____

Directions: Read this passage about how to make a mummy. Then answer questions 11–20.

How to Make a Mummy

The ancient Egyptians are famous for making mummies. But it took them centuries to perfect their techniques and figure out the best ways to preserve their dead. Their methods were so good that we are still finding Egyptian mummies today! Embalmers performed the mummification process. It was complex, took many days, and always began the same way—with a corpse! Here's how they did it.

> What kind of a passage is this?

1. Wash the body with palm wine and water from the Nile River.

2. Make an incision on the left side of the abdomen.

3. Remove the lungs, stomach, liver, and intestines through the incision. Cover them with a kind of salt called *natron*.

4. Push a brain hook up into the left nostril and jiggle it around to liquefy the brain.

5. Turn the body over and allow the brain to flow out through the nostrils and into a bowl.

6. Place the preserved liver, lungs, stomach, and intestines in canopic jars.

7. Cover the body in natron.

8. After 40 days, remove the natron. The body will be darker and much thinner.

9. Wash the body. If available, stuff the cavity with resin.

10. Call the makeup artist to apply makeup to the face. He may also fit the deceased with a wig.

11. Rub the body in scented oil.

> Mummification is a long and complex process. Read each step carefully.

12. Brush the body in melted pine resin (sap) to seal it.

13. Place a golden plate with a Wadjet eye (the eye of Horus) over the incision.

| Test A | Name: _____ |

How to Make a Mummy *(cont.)*

14. Waft incense to purify the air.

15. Wrap the body in strips of linen.

16. Insert amulets (charms) in between the layers of linens.

17. Place a vulture amulet at the throat of the deceased.

18. Place a special amulet called a "heart scarab" over the heart.

19. Place a mask over the face of the deceased.

20. Label the deceased with their name.

21. Place the mummy in a sarcophagus.

22. Place the sarcophagus in a tomb.

Voilà! Mummy!

After the mummy was made, the ancient Egyptians would recite spells or prayers from the *Egyptian Book of the Dead* to help the deceased in the afterlife.

Questions 11–20: Select the best answer.

11. Who performed the mummification process?

    A. priests

    B. embalmers

    C. Horus

    D. a mummy doctor

Type of Question: _____

Go back to the first paragraph of the passage to locate the answer.

Test A	Name: _____

How to Make a Mummy *(cont.)*

12. What is an incision?

    A. a mummy

    B. a type of preserving salt

    C. part of the abdomen

    D. a long cut

> Look at step 3 to see how the incision is used.

Type of Question: _____

13. What would be the best reason that the ancient Egyptians liquefied the brain?

    A. It was easier to preserve in this form.

    B. It was the only way to get it out of the skull.

    C. It was drunk by the embalmers.

    D. None of these.

> Consider the types of tools the ancient Egyptians had and what the brain is encased in.

Type of Question: _____

14. Most likely, why didn't the ancient Egyptians preserve the brain?

    A. They didn't think it was very important.

    B. It was too big to fit into a canopic jar.

    C. They couldn't store liquids.

    D. The brain was considered sacred.

> Think about how you treat something that you value.

Type of Question: _____

15. Which organ is not removed?

    A. the stomach

    B. the heart

    C. the liver

    D. the lungs

> What organ listed is not stored in a canopic jar?

16. Where is the Wadjet eye placed?

    A. in between layers of linens

    B. under the face mask

    C. over the incision

    D. in the sarcophagus

> Point Right To It!

Type of Question: _____

Test A   Name: _____

How to Make a Mummy *(cont.)*

17. What part of the mummification process took the longest?

    A. step 8

    B. step 22

    C. step 3

    D. step 4

> Go back and review the steps listed.

18. What is pine resin used for?

    A. to dry out the body

    B. to scent the body

    C. to identify the body

    D. to seal the body

> Point Right To It!

Type of Question: _____

19. What do the embalmers do just before they wrap the body in linen?

    A. place the Wadjet eye over the incision

    B. purify the air

    C. place the vulture amulet at the throat

    D. brush the body in natron

> Review steps 14 and 15.

20. Which of the following terms is closest to the meaning of *sarcophagus*?

    A. mausoleum

    B. pyramid

    C. coffin

    D. linen

> Visualize a sarcophagus to help you make a connection.

Type of Question: _____

Test A   Name: _____

Directions: Read this poem about baseball. Then answer questions 21–30.

Casey at the Bat
by
Ernest Lawrence Thayer

The Outlook wasn't brilliant for the Mudville Nine that day:
The score stood four to two, with but one inning more to play.
And then when Cooney died at first, and Barrows did the same,
A sickly silence fell upon the patrons of the game.

A straggling few got up to go deeper in despair. The rest
Clung to that hope which springs eternal in the human breast;
They thought, if only Casey could get but a whack at that—
We'd put up even money, now, with Casey at the bat.

> What is happening in this poem?

But Flynn preceded Casey, as did also Jimmy Blake,
And the former was a lulu and the latter was a cake;
So upon that stricken multitude grim melancholy sat,
For there seemed but little chance of Casey's getting to the bat.

But Flynn let drive a single, to the wonderment of all,
And Blake, the much despised, tore the cover off the ball;
And when the dust lifted, and the men saw what had occurred,
There was Jimmy safe at second and Flynn a-hugging third.

Then from 5,000 throats and more there rose a lusty yell;
It rumbled through the valley, it rattled in the dell;
It knocked upon the mountain and recoiled upon the flat;
For Casey, mighty Casey, was advancing to the bat.

> How does the crowd feel about what is happening to their team?

There was an ease in Casey's manner as he stepped into his place;
There was a pride in Casey's bearing and a smile on Casey's face.
And when, responding to the cheers, he lightly doffed his hat,
No stranger in the crowd could doubt 'twas Casey at the bat.

Ten thousand eyes were on him as he rubbed his hands with dirt
Five thousand tongues applauded when he wiped them on his shirt.
Then while the writhing pitcher ground the ball into his hip,
Defiance gleamed in Casey's eye, a sneer curled Casey's lip.

Test A   Name: _____

Casey at the Bat *(cont.)*

And now the leather-covered sphere came hurtling through the air,
And Casey stood a-watching it in haughty grandeur there.
Close by the sturdy batsman the ball unheeded sped—
"That ain't my style," said Casey. "Strike one," the umpire said.

From the benches, black with people, there went up a muffled roar,
Like the beating of the storm-waves on a stern and distant shore.
"Kill him! Kill the umpire!" shouted someone on the stand;
And its likely they'd a-killed him had not Casey raised his hand.

With a smile of Christian charity great Casey's visage shone;
He stilled the rising tumult; he bade the game go on;
He signaled to the pitcher, and once more the spheroid flew;
But Casey still ignored it, and the umpire said, "Strike two."

> What does Casey's behavior reveal about the kind of person he is?

"Fraud!" cried the maddened thousands, and echo answered fraud;
But one scornful look from Casey and the audience was awed.
They saw his face grow stern and cold, they saw his muscles strain,
And they knew that Casey wouldn't let that ball go by again.

The sneer is gone from Casey's lip, his teeth are clenched in hate;
He pounds with cruel violence his bat upon the plate.
And now the pitcher holds the ball, and now he lets it go.
And now the air is shattered by the force of Casey's blow.

> Do the Mudville Nine win or lose the game?

Oh, somewhere in this favored land the sun is shining bright;
The band is playing somewhere, and somewhere hearts are light;
And somewhere men are laughing, and somewhere children shout;
But there is no joy in Mudville—mighty Casey has struck out.

Test A   Name: _____

Casey at the Bat *(cont.)*

Questions 21–30: Select the best answer.

21. What is the rhyme scheme in this poem?

    A. abab

    B. aabb

    C. abca

    D. baba

> Look for the pattern of lines in each stanza that rhymes

22. What are the Mudville Nine?

    A. a group of angry spectators

    B. a baseball team

    C. the town leaders

    D. a Little League team

> Look for vocabulary that is associated with a particular sport.

23. How many people were watching the game?

    A. 10,000

    B. The poem doesn't say.

    C. 5,000

    D. 9

> Point Right To It!

24. Which of the following adjectives best describes Casey?

    A. intimidated

    B. terrified

    C. confident

    D. nervous

> Go back and read stanza six to see how the poet describes Casey.

Type of Question: _____

25. The crowd yelling "Kill the umpire!" is an example of

    A. simile.

    B. onomatopoeia.

    C. hyperbole.

    D. allusion.

> Look for the option that means "exaggeration."

Test A   Name: _____

Casey at the Bat *(cont.)*

26. What is the leather-covered sphere referred to in the poem?

    A. the bat

    B. the umpire

    C. Flynn

    D. the ball

> Go back and reread stanza eight.

27. What type of poem is Casey at the Bat?

    A. ballad

    B. sonnet

    C. cinquain

    D. limerick

> Use the process of elimination to find the correct answer.

28. Why is there no joy in Mudville?

    A. It rained during the entire game.

    B. Casey got injured.

    C. The Mudville Nine lost the game.

    D. Some spectators began to leave the stadium.

> Think about the event in the poem.

29. How many batters were up at bat before Casey?

    A. 4

    B. 2

    C. 6

    D. 5

> Go back and count the number of players that batted before Casey.

Type of Question: _____

30. From whose point of view is this poem written?

    A. the umpire

    B. Casey

    C. a spectator sympathetic to the Mudville Nine

    D. a spectator sympathetic to the team opposing the Mudville Nine

> Think about how the narrator feels about the event he describes.

WALNUT HILL LINE Train Schedule

Test A — TO CENTER CITY: MONDAYS through FRIDAYS (Except MAJOR HOLIDAYS)

Fare Zone	Stations	812	814	816	818	982	822	714	830	822	912	918	932	909	841	810	852
		AM	AM	AM	AM	AM	AM	AM	AM/PM	PM	PM	PM	PM	PM	PM	PM	PM
2	Walnut Hill	7:07	7:38	8:11	8:36	T9:07	T9:57	10:57	11:58	12:52	1:51	2:51	3:34	4:33	5:22	5:53	6:17
2	Highland	7:08	7:39	8:12	8:37	F9:08	F9:58	10:58	11:59	12:53	1:52	2:52	3:35	4:34	5:23	5:54	6:19
2	Seven Sisters	7:10	7:41	8:14	8:39	9:10	9:59	10:59	12:01	12:54	1:53	2:53	3:36	4:35	5:24	5:55	6:20
2	Allen Lane	7:12	7:43	8:16	8:41	9:12	10:01	11:01	12:02	12:56	1:55	2:55	3:38	4:37	5:26	5:57	6:22
2	Carpenter Station	7:14	7:45	8:18	8:43	9:14	10:02	11:02	12:03	12:57	1:56	2:56	3:39	4:38	5:27	5:58	T6:23
2	Summit	7:16	7:47	8:20	8:45	9:16	10:03	11:03	12:05	12:58	1:57	2:57	3:40	4:39	5:28	5:59	6:24
2	Valley Green	7:18	7:49	8:22	8:47	9:18	10:05	11:05	12:07	1:00	1:59	2:59	3:42	4:41	5:30	6:01	6:26
1	Chilton	7:20	7:51	8:24	8:49	9:20	10:07	11:07	12:09	1:02	2:01	3:01	3:44	4:43	5:32	6:03	6:28
1	Queen Lane	7:22	7:53	8:26	8:51	9:22	10:09	11:09	12:12	1:04	2:03	3:03	3:46	4:45	5:34	6:05	6:30
1	North Madison	7:25	7:56	8:29			10:12	11:12	12:24	F1:07	F2:06	F3:06	3:49	4:48	5:37	6:08	
C	30th Street Station	7:36	8:08	8:41	9:06	9:35	10:24	11:24	12:29	1:18	2:18	3:18	4:01	5:03	5:51	6:20	6:43
C	Suburban Station	7:41	8:13	8:46	9:11	9:40	10:29	11:29	12:34	1:24	2:23	3:23	4:08	5:08	5:56	6:25	6:48
C	Center City	7:46	8:18	8:51	9:16	9:45	10:34	11:34	12:38	1:29	2:28	3:28	4:13	5:13	6:01	6:30	6:53

Review each section of the train schedule carefully.

T — This train stops to discharge and pick up passengers but may depart ahead of schedule.

F — This train stops to discharge passengers on notice to conductor and picks up passengers standing on platform in position visible to engineer.

☐ — If no time appears, the train does not make a stop at the station.

General Information

Schedule Times: Indicate when train departs from station

Fare Payment Options: cash, tickets, passes. Please check the Fare Guide on the website for complete fare information.

Quiet Ride Car: Available on all weekday trains (Monday–Friday 4:00 a.m.–7:00 p.m.) with 3 or more cars open for passenger service. The first car will be designated as your Quiet Ride Car.

Rail Major Holidays: New Year's Day, Memorial Day, 4th of July, Labor Day, Thanksgiving Day, Christmas Day

WALNUT HILL LINE Train Schedule *(cont.)*

Test A   **TO WALNUT HILL: MONDAYS through FRIDAYS (Except MAJOR HOLIDAYS)**

Fare Zone	Train Number / Stations	609 AM	452 AM	223 AM	976 AM	521 AM	297 AM	883 AM	830 AM/PM	147 PM	319 PM	676 PM	287 PM	111 PM	995 PM	217 PM	457 PM
C	Center City	6:43	7:13	7:41	8:13	8:47	9:38	10:07	11:50	12:50	1:50	2:36	3:32	4:13	4:36	5:12	5:46
C	Suburban Station	6:48	7:18	7:46	8:18	8:52	9:43	10:42	11:55	12:55	1:55	2:41	3:37	4:18	4:41	5:17	5:51
C	30th Street Station	6:52	7:22	7:50	8:22	8:56	9:47	10:46	11:59	12:59	1:59	2:45	3:41	4:22	4:45	5:21	5:55
1	North Madison	7:04		8:05		9:07	9:59	10:58	12:11	F1:11	F2:11	F2:57	3:53	4:34	4:57	5:33	6:07
1	Queen Lane	7:07	7:37	8:08	8:37	9:10	10:02	11:01	12:14	1:14	2:14	3:00	3:56	4:37	5:00	5:36	6:10
1	Chilton	7:09	7:39	8:11	8:39	9:12	10:04	11:03	12:16	1:16	2:16	3:02	3:58	4:39	5:02	5:38	6:12
2	Valley Green	7:10	7:40	8:12	8:40	9:13	10:05	11:04	12:17	1:17	2:17	3:03	3:59	4:40	5:03	5:40	6:14
2	Summit	7:11	7:41	8:13	8:41	9:14	10:06	11:05	12:18	1:18	2:18	3:04	4:01	4:42	5:05	5:42	6:16
2	Carpenter Station	7:13	7:43	8:15	8:43	9:16	10:08	11:07	12:20	1:20	2:20	3:06	4:03	4:44	5:07	5:44	T6:18
2	Allen Lane	7:14	7:45	8:17	8:45	9:18	10:10	11:09	12:22	1:22	2:22	3:08	4:05	4:46	5:09	5:46	6:20
2	Seven Sisters	7:16	7:47	8:19	8:47	9:20	10:12	11:11	12:24	1:24	2:24	3:10	4:07	4:48	5:11	5:48	6:22
2	Highland	7:17	7:49	8:21	8:49	F9:21	10:13	11:12	12:25	1:25	2:25	3:11	4:09	4:50	5:13	5:50	6:24
2	Walnut Hill	7:20	7:52	8:24	T8:52	T9:24	10:16	11:15	12:28	1:28	2:28	3:14	4:12	4:53	5:16	5:53	6:27

T — This train stops to discharge and pick up passengers but may depart ahead of schedule.

F — This train stops to discharge passengers on notice to conductor and picks up passengers standing on platform in position visible to engineer.

☐ — If no time appears, the train does not make a stop at the station.

What kind of information does the schedule provide?

General Information

Schedule Times: Indicate when train departs from station

Fare Payment Options: cash, tickets, passes. Please check the Fare Guide on the website for complete fare information.

Quiet Ride Car: Available on all weekday trains (Monday–Friday 4:00 a.m.–7:00 p.m.) with 3 or more cars open for passenger service. The first car will be designated as your Quiet Ride Car.

Rail Major Holidays: New Year's Day, Memorial Day, 4th of July, Labor Day, Thanksgiving Day, Christmas Day

Test A | Name: _____

WALNUT HILL LINE Train Schedule *(cont.)*

Questions 31–40: Select the best answer.

31. Which station is the farthest from Center City?

    A. Suburban Station

    B. North Madison

    C. Seven Sisters

    D. Walnut Hill

> Look at the first and last stop on the schedule.

32. If you got on the train at North Madison at 4:34, what time would you arrive at Seven Sisters?

    A. 4:48

    B. 4:37

    C. 4:34

    D. 4:35

> Point Right To It!

33. What do the blank boxes on the schedule mean?

    A. The printers of the schedule made a mistake.

    B. The train doesn't stop at the station.

    C. The train makes unscheduled stops at the station.

    D. Passengers can get off the train at this station but not on it.

> Use the information below the schedule to help answer this question.

Type of Question: _____

34. If you take the 1:59 from Valley Green to Center City, how long will you be on the train?

    A. 29 minutes

    B. 30 minutes

    C. It depends on how fast the train is moving.

    D. 2 hours and 28 minutes

> This is a simple addition problem.

35. What do you think the Quiet Ride Car is?

    A. A railroad car that is soundproofed.

    B. A railroad car that makes very little noise.

    C. The car where talking on cell phones and to other passengers is discouraged.

    D. The car where people talk quietly.

> Think of other places where there is quiet and what that usually means.

Type of Question: _____

Test A   Name: _____

WALNUT HILL LINE Train Schedule *(cont.)*

36. What makes the F9:21 from Highland to Walnut Hill different than most of the trains?

    A. It won't stop unless someone wants to get on or off of the train.

    B. It may leave the train station ahead of schedule.

    C. It is usually late.

    D. It doesn't have a Quiet Ride Car.

> Review what the codes on the schedule mean.

37. If you get on the 11:02 at the Carpenter Station, what will the next stop be?

    A. Allen Lane

    B. Summit

    C. Walnut Hill

    D. Center City

> Make sure you are looking at the schedule going to Center City.

38. Which of the following is not a rail major holiday?

    A. New Year's Day

    B. Memorial Day

    C. President's Day

    D. Thanksgiving Day

> Review the Rail Major Holidays section.

39. Where is the Quiet Ride Car located?

    A. last car on the train

    B. middle car on the train

    C. third car on the train

    D. first car on the train

> Review the Quiet Ride Car section.

Type of Question: _____

40. Why does it take the 6:05 from Queen Lane 2 minutes longer to get to Center City than the 6:30 train?

    A. There is more traffic at 6:30.

    B. The conductor of the 6:05 drives slower than the other conductors.

    C. It is probably a misprint on the schedule.

    D. The 6:30 train doesn't stop at North Madison.

> Implicit questions often begin with the word *why*.

Type of Question: _____

Test A   Name: _____

Directions: Read the retelling of the classic story "The Gift of the Magi." Then answer questions 41–50.

The Gift of the Magi
by
O. Henry

One dollar and eighty-seven cents. That was all. And sixty cents of it was in pennies. Pennies saved one and two at a time by bulldozing the grocer and the vegetable man and the butcher until one's cheeks burned with the silent embarrassment and shame. Three times Della counted it. One dollar and eighty-seven cents. And the next day would be Christmas. There was clearly nothing left to do but flop down on the shabby little couch and howl. So Della did it. Which left Della to believe that life is made up of sobs, sniffles, and smiles, but mostly sniffles.

> At what time of year is this story set?

While Della continues to cry on the couch, let's take a look at her home. It is a furnished apartment that costs $8 per week. It could have been worse, but it certainly could have been better, too. The mail-slot was so old that it was rusted shut, and the electric buzzer hadn't worked in over six months. But Della and her husband, James Dillingham Young, loved each other very much. Even though times were hard and they were poor, they were happy because they had each other.

Della finished her cry and blotted her eyes with a tissue. She stood by the window and looked out dully at a gray cat walking a gray fence in a gray backyard. Tomorrow would be Christmas Day, and she had only $1.87 with which to buy Jim a present. She had been saving every penny she could for months, with this result. Twenty dollars a week doesn't go far. Expenses had been greater than she had calculated. They always are. Only $1.87 to buy a present for Jim. Her Jim. Many a happy hour she had spent planning for something nice for him. Something fine and rare and sterling—something just a little bit near to being worthy of the honor of being owned by Jim.

> How does the author use language to create the tone of the story?

There was a pier-glass between the windows of the room. Perhaps you have seen a pier-glass before. A very thin and very agile person may, by observing his reflection in a rapid sequence of longitudinal strips, obtain a fairly accurate conception of his looks. Della, being slender, had mastered the art. Suddenly she whirled from the window and stood before the glass. Her eyes were shining brilliantly, but her face had lost its color within twenty seconds. Rapidly she pulled down her hair and let it fall to its full length.

Test A	Name: _____

The Gift of the Magi *(cont.)*

Now, there were two possessions of the James Dillingham Youngs in which they both took a mighty pride. One was Jim's gold watch that had been his father's and his grandfather's. The other was Della's hair. Had the Queen of Sheba lived in the apartment across the airshaft, Della would have let her hair hang out the window just to try to make her jealous. Had King Tut been the janitor, with all his treasures piled up in the basement, Jim would have pulled out his watch every time he passed, just to see him pluck at his beard from envy.

So now Della's beautiful hair fell about her rippling and shining like a cascade of brown waters. It reached below her knee and made itself almost a garment of her. And then she did it up again nervously and quickly. She faltered for a minute and stood still while a tear or two splashed on the worn red carpet.

· · · · · · · · · · · · · ·
· Why does Della cry? ·
· · · · · · · · · · · · · ·

On went her old brown jacket and brown hat. With a whirl of skirts and with the brilliant sparkle still in her eyes, she fluttered out the door and down the stairs to the street.

Where she stopped the sign read: "Madame Sofronie. Hair Goods of All Kinds." One flight up Della ran, and collected herself, panting. Madame Sofronie was a stern looking woman.

"Will you buy my hair?" Della asked.

"I buy hair," said Madame. "Take your hat off and let's have a sight at the looks of it."

Down rippled the brown cascade.

"Twenty dollars," said Madame lifting the mass with a practiced hand.

"Give it to me quick," said Della.

For the next two hours, Della was ransacking the stores for Jim's present. She found it at last. It was a platinum chain on which Jim could attach his prized pocket watch. As soon as she saw it, she knew that it must be Jim's. It was like him. Twenty-one dollars they took from her for it, and she hurried home with the eighty-seven cents. With that chain on his watch, Jim might be properly anxious about the time in any company. Grand as the watch was, he sometimes looked at it on the sly on account of the old leather strap that he used in place of a chain.

Test A Name: _____

The Gift of the Magi *(cont.)*

When Della reached home she got out her curling irons and lighted the gas and went to work repairing the ravages made by generosity added to love. Within forty minutes her head was covered with tiny, close-lying curls that made her look like a little boy.

Della set the watch chain on the corner of the table near the door. She heard his step on the stair and whispered to herself, "Please God, make him love me just the same." The door opened and Jim stepped in and closed it. He looked thin and very serious. Poor fellow, he needed a new overcoat and he was without gloves.

Jim fixed his eyes on Della. There was an expression in them that she could not read, and it terrified her. It was not anger, nor surprise, nor disapproval, nor horror, nor any of the sentiments that she had been prepared for. He simply stared at her with that peculiar expression on his face.

Della wriggled off the table and went for him.

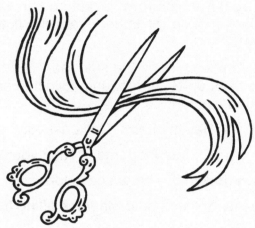

"Jim, darling," she cried, "don't look at me that way. I had my hair cut off and sold because I couldn't have lived through Christmas without giving you a present. It'll grow out again—you won't mind, will you? I just had to do it. My hair grows awfully fast. Say 'Merry Christmas!' Jim, and let's be happy. You don't know what a nice—what a beautiful, nice gift I've got you."

"You've cut off your hair?" asked Jim, laboriously, as if he had not arrived at that patent fact yet even after the hardest mental labor.

"Cut it off and sold it," said Della. "Don't you like me just as well, anyhow? I'm me without my hair, ain't I?"

Jim looked about the room curiously.

"You say your hair is gone?" he said, with an almost idiotic air.

"You needn't look for it," said Della. "It's sold, I tell you—sold and gone, too."

Jim drew a package from his overcoat pocket and threw it upon the table.

"Don't make any mistake, Della," he said, "about me. I don't think there's anything in the way of a haircut or a shave or a shampoo that could make me like my girl any less. But if you unwrap that package you may see why you had me going at first."

How do you think Jim feels about Della's short hair?

Test A   Name: _____

The Gift of the Magi *(cont.)*

Della's nimble fingers tore at the string and paper. And then an ecstatic scream of joy. For there lay The Combs—the set of combs, side and back, that Della had worshipped long in a Broadway window. Beautiful combs, pure tortoise shell she yearned for without the least hope of possession. And now, they were all hers, but the tresses that should have been adorned by the coveted adornments were gone.

But she hugged them and said: "My hair grows so fast, Jim!"

And then Della leapt up and eagerly gave Jim her watch chain.

"Isn't it dandy, Jim? Give me your watch. I want to see how it looks on it."

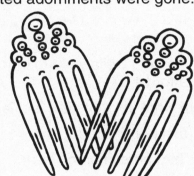

Jim kind of laughed and said, "I sold the watch to get the money to buy your combs."

Here I have related to you the events of people in an apartment who sacrificed for each other the greatest treasures in their house. They each gave away what they most treasured to make the one they loved happy. This is the true meaning of Christmas.

Questions 41–50: Select the best answer.

41. When do you think this story is set?

   A. in the present day

   B. in the future

   C. about 100 years ago

   D. about 200 years ago

Look for clues in the story that can help you rule out three of these options.

Type of Question: _____

42. How are the main characters related?

   A. They are brother and sister.

   B. They are husband and wife.

   C. They are father and daughter.

   D. They are mother and son.

Go back and read the second paragraph.

Test A   Name: _____

The Gift of the Magi *(cont.)*

43. What is the problem in the story?

  A. Della and Jim don't have enough money for the rent.

  B. The doorbell is broken.

  C. It is a harsh winter, and Jim doesn't have a coat or gloves.

  D. Jim and Della want to buy gifts for each other but can't afford it.

> Think of what the characters want and what is stopping them from getting it.

44. From what point of view is this story told?

  A. first person

  B. third person omniscient

  C. third person limited

  D. second person

> How much does the narrator know about what the characters think and feel?

45. What words best describe Della's mood at the beginning of the story?

  A. joyful and patient

  B. frustrated and sad

  C. angry and depressed

  D. envious and sad

> Consider Della's thoughts and actions.

Type of Question: _____

46. In paragraph 6, the reader learns that Della "faltered for a minute and stood still while a tear or two splashed on the worn red carpet." Why is Della crying?

  A. because she is poor

  B. because she knows she is going to cut her hair

  C. because she is worried about Jim

  D. because she can't afford to buy Jim the watch chain

> What is Della doing as she cries?

Type of Question: _____

Test A   Name: _____

The Gift of the Magi *(cont.)*

47. How much does Madame Sofronie pay for Della's hair?

  A. 21 dollars

  B. $1.87

  (C.) 20 dollars

  D. 35 dollars

Type of Question: _____

48. The author describes the combs as "coveted adornments." What does *coveted* mean?

  A. beautiful

  B. expensive

  C. rare

  (D.) strongly desired

49. What is the theme of the story?

  (A.) sacrifice to give to others

  B. duty to your family

  C. the injustice of poverty

  D. the anger of envy

50. Why is the resolution in the story an example of irony?

  (A.) Della and Jim gave each other gifts that they can no longer use.

  B. The sacrifices they made for each other are meaningless.

  C. They are still poor.

  D. Because Della says her hair will grow back fast.

Point Right To It!

Go back and read the word in context to determine the meaning.

Think about what the characters do and why they do it to help you determine the theme.

Irony often includes the element of surprise.

Test B   Name: _____

Directions: Read the passage called "The Night Sky." Then answer questions 1–10.

The Night Sky

When you observe the night sky on a clear evening, there are certain objects that you might see with the naked eye. The *naked eye* means without the use of a telescope. First, the night sky is full of trillions and trillions of stars. Of course, you don't see that many. In fact, the stars that are visible to us on Earth represent only a very tiny portion of all of the stars that exist in the universe.

❖ **Types of Stars**

Stars come in different sizes, magnitudes, and temperatures. The magnitude of a star is its brightness. Scientists use a measure called *absolute magnitude* to tell how bright a star really is. Absolute magnitude describes how bright the star would appear if it were the same distance from Earth as our sun. The absolute magnitude of our sun is 4.8. The next closest star to Earth is Proxima Centauri. It has an absolute magnitude of 15.53. You can tell which stars are brighter or less bright than our sun by learning their absolute magnitude.

> Scan the headings and subheading before you read.

Scientists also study the temperature of stars. The classification system for stars, according to temperature is O, B, A, F, G, K, and M. Scientists have a funny sentence to help them remember the system. It is *Oh, Be A Fine Guy/Girl, Kiss Me!* In this system, O-class stars are the hottest, and M-class stars are the coolest.

The temperature of a star affects how it appears in the sky. Some stars glow white, while others shine yellow, blue, or red. Our sun is a G-class star, which as we all know, shines bright yellow.

Star Classification Table		
Star Type	**Color**	**Approximate Surface Temperature**
O	Blue	Over 25,000 K
B	Blue	11,000–25,000 K
A	Blue	7,500–11,000 K
F	Blue to White	6,000–7,500 K
G	White to Yellow	5,000–6,000 K
K	Orange to Red	3,500–5,000 K
M	Red	Under 3,500 K

Note: Temperature is measured in Kelvin (K).

| Test B | Name: _____ |

The Night Sky *(cont.)*

❖ The Moon

The moon is a natural satellite of Earth. It is also the object in the sky that is the closest to Earth. The moon is 238,857 miles from Earth. The first man landed on the moon in 1969. His name was Neil Armstrong.

While the moon itself does not change in size or shape, it appears differently to us on Earth at different times in a month. These differences are called the phases of the moon. They are a result of the sun shining on only half of the moon at a single time.

Our moon has been the subject of many books, movies, and folklore. There is a myth that when the moon is full, it can transform people into werewolves. Some tall tales claim that the moon is made of Swiss cheese because from our vantage point, it looks like it is full of holes. There are still other stories that claim there is a man who lives on the moon!

There have also been many famous songs sung about the moon, including: "Fly Me to the Moon," "Moon River," "Blue Moon," "Shine on Harvest Moon," "Howlin' at the Moon," and "It's Only a Paper Moon."

> Review all of the phases of the moon.

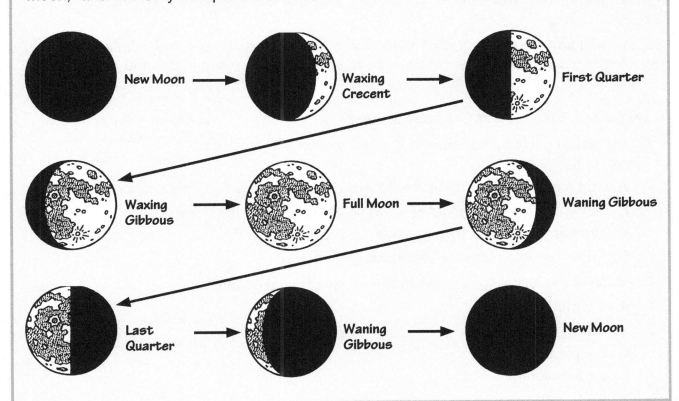

New Moon → Waxing Crecent → First Quarter

Waxing Gibbous → Full Moon → Waning Gibbous

Last Quarter → Waning Gibbous → New Moon

Test B	Name: _____

The Night Sky *(cont.)*

❖ Other Objects in the Night Sky

Planets

There are a few planets in our solar system that we can see at night. Venus is often called the morning or evening star because it shines the brightest at sunrise and sunset. We can also see Mercury, Jupiter, and Saturn.

Comets

Comets are small, icy objects that go hurtling through the solar system. When they streak across the sky, it often looks like they have a tail. Comets are seen very rarely. The most famous comet is called Halley's Comet, which makes an appearance about every 75 years.

Meteoroids

A meteoroid is a chunk of rock like a boulder. Sometimes you can see them shooting across the sky. Meteoroids are often called shooting stars for this very reason. A meteor is the path or streak that the meteoroid makes as it blasts through the sky.

Meteoroids are rare, but sometimes you can see a whole lot of them together. This event is called a meteor shower. There is a famous one that takes place every year called the Leonids. This shower is so spectacular that it is called the *King of Meteor Showers*.

So, the next time you find yourself outside on a clear, cloudless evening, take a look up. Maybe you will see a star twinkling blue, a waxing moon, or a meteoroid hurtling towards planet Earth.

Questions 1–10: Select the best answer.

> Go back and reread the *Types of Stars* section.

1. How would you best summarize the information in the *Types of Stars* section?

    A. The night sky is full of different kinds of stars that we can only see a portion of.

    B. Many objects in the night sky can be observed with the naked eye.

    C. Stars are classified by magnitude and temperature.

    D. There are lots of myths surrounding our moon.

2. Which of the following is possible to see with the naked eye?

    A. a virus

    B. a dust mite

    > Make a deduction.

    C. the planet Neptune

    D. an earthworm

Test B   Name: _____

The Night Sky *(cont.)*

3. If a star has an absolute magnitude of 3.5, is it brighter or less bright than the sun?

    A. brighter

    B. less bright

    C. the same brightness

    D. not enough information is provided

> Review the meaning of absolute magnitude.

4. What is O B A F G K M?

    A. the classification system for absolute magnitude

    B. the phases of the moon

    C. the classification system for the distance of stars from Earth

    D. the classification of stars by temperature

> Scan the passage until you find the letters in the question, then reread.

5. A K-class star glows

    A. orange to red.

    B. yellow.

    C. blue.

    D. blue to white.

> Review the Star Classification Table.

Type of Question: _____

6. The first and last quarter moons can be best described as

    A. full moons.

    B. half moons.

    C. crescent-shaped moons.

    D. new moons.

> Review the diagram of the phases of the moon.

7. What causes the phases of the moon?

    A. the rotation of the moon

    B. the closeness of the moon to Earth

    C. the magnitude of the sun

    D. the sun shining on only half of the moon at a single time

> Scan the section about moon phases.

Type of Question: _____

Test B   Name: _____

The Night Sky *(cont.)*

8. How does the author organize this passage?

    A. headings and subheadings

    B. cause and effect

    C. index glossary

    D. paragraphs

> Use the process of elimination.

9. Most likely, why has the moon been the subject of so many songs and folklore?

    A. Many words rhyme with *moon*.

    B. Many people have been there.

    C. Everyone can see it, but most people have not been there.

    D. It is close.

> Implicit questions often include the word *why*.

Type of Question: _____

10. What is the difference between a *comet* and *meteoroid*?

    A. A comet is rare; a meteoroid is common.

    B. A comet makes a streak called a meteor, a meteoroid doesn't.

    C. A meteoroid is made of ice; a comet is made of rock.

    D. A comet is made of ice; a meteoroid is made of rock.

> Review the section to make sure you understand the differences.

Test B   Name: _____

Directions: Read the passage called "Galileo: Father of Modern Science." Then answer questions 11–20.

Galileo: Father of Modern Science

Galileo Galilei was a superstar of the Renaissance. The Renaissance was a time when people rediscovered the world of the ancient Greeks and Romans. They prized those great thinkers of the past. This time period is also called the *Age of Enlightenment*. It is called this because so many great scientists and inventors lived and worked during that time. Galileo is one of those people. He was born in Florence, Italy, in 1564. Florence was the ground zero of the Renaissance. In fact, the Renaissance was born in Florence. So, Galileo arrived in the right place at the right time!

> Who was Galileo and why was he so important?

Young Galileo

When Galileo was young he thought about being a priest. The church was the center of life for most people in the 16th century. Like many people of his time, his faith was important to him. But Galileo's father wanted his son to go to the University of Pisa. He wanted him to study medicine. Just like today, becoming a doctor was a good way to earn a living. Once Galileo arrived at school he became interested in math. He never became a doctor. In 1588, at the age of 24, he became a teacher at an important school in Pisa.

> Look at how the passage is organized.

Galileo taught in Pisa for about four years. Then his father died. This meant that Galileo had to take care of his younger brother. Galileo moved to the city of Padua. He took a job as a math teacher. Even though events beyond his control brought Galileo to Padua, he did some of his most important work there.

The Telescope

Before the time of Galileo, the only way astronomers could view the sky was with the naked eye. There was a kind of basic telescope, but it was not very good. In 1608, Galileo built a telescope that was much better for viewing the night sky. The first telescope he made magnified objects by three times. The next one he made was more powerful. It made objects look thirty times larger.

The new telescope changed everything. A few short years after it was made, Galileo used it to discover four of the moons of Jupiter. He named the moons Io, Europa, Ganymede, and Callisto. Today, they are called the Galilean moons, because Galileo was the first one to see them!

Test B	Name: _____

Galileo: Father of Modern Science (cont.)

The Telescope (cont.)

People were amazed at his discovery. Many didn't believe it! At that time, people thought that all of the objects in the sky orbited Earth. But there was Galileo with his spyglass proving that there are objects in the sky that orbit planets!

Galileo was the first to see some other features of our solar system that were not known at the time. He saw Saturn and Neptune. At first he thought that the rings around Saturn were hundreds of tiny planets. Galileo also saw that the planet Venus goes through phases like our moon. This helped to prove a theory about how our solar system works. For a long time, people thought that Earth was at the center of the solar system. But Galileo's observation helped to show that the body in the center of the solar system is the sun. He wrote a book about this that would land him in some trouble with the church.

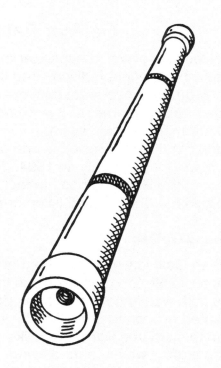

Controversy

The idea that the sun was at the center of the solar system was not what the church taught. The church believed that Earth was at the center of the universe. Galileo was faithful and loyal to the church, but he was also a scientist.

> What did Galileo do that angered the church?

He had looked up into the sky with his telescope, and he saw things that proved that this teaching was not correct. But the church was very powerful, and the leaders had Galileo arrested. He was given a trial to defend his position about what was at the center of the solar system, but he lost. He was convicted of a crime called *heresy*. He was placed under house arrest for the remainder of his life.

This has happened often in the history of ideas. Sometimes, religious belief and science conflict with each other. There was a time when people believed that Earth was flat. They thought that if you sailed too far, you would fall off the edge. In the 17th century, many people were burned at the stake because they were thought to have practiced witchcraft. Sometimes it is hard for people to accept new scientific evidence. It takes time. This is what happened to Galileo. He defended a scientific theory that today no one would argue with. But in his day, it was controversial. For this reason, Galileo is said to have been ahead of his time.

Test B **Name:** _____

Galileo: Father of Modern Science *(cont.)*

Legacy

The church allowed Galileo to live under house arrest. That meant that he lived in his home. He was able to write and do research as long as he stayed away from the topic that caused the initial problem. During this time, Galileo wrote several important works about physics that had a big impact on future scientists.

Galileo made a huge contribution to both astronomy and physics. He is hailed as the Father of Modern Science and is one of the most important scientific thinkers of all time. He died in 1642 at the age of 77.

Questions 11–20: Select the best answer.

11. What era most likely came right before the Renaissance?

    A. The Age of Reason

    B. The Industrial Age

    C. The Dark Ages

    D. The Royal Age

Type of Question: _____

> Think about other terms for the Renaissance.

12. Why does the author refer to Florence as the *ground zero* of the Renaissance?

    A. Because there was a terrorist attack there.

    B. Because Florence is where the Renaissance began.

    C. Because Florence was in the center of the Italian peninsula.

    D. Because so many great scientists were born there.

> Implicit questions usually begin with *why*.

13. What is the difference between the first and second types of telescopes that Galileo built?

    A. The first telescope didn't work, the second one did.

    B. The second one was much more powerful than the first.

    C. The first one was more powerful than the second.

    D. The first one magnified objects by 30 times.

Type of Question: _____

> Use the subtitles to help you find this information.

Test B   Name: _____

Galileo: Father of Modern Science *(cont.)*

14. What is a *spyglass*?

   A. another word for telescope

   B. something you watch people through

   C. the nickname of Galileo's first telescope

   D. the type of material that the telescope was made from

> Review the context in which this word is used.

15. What is Europa?

   A. a moon of Jupiter

   B. a continent in the Western Hemisphere

   C. a large sunspot

   D. the name of the university where Galileo taught

> Point Right To It!

Type of Question: _____

16. Why was the discovery of the phases of Venus important?

   A. It proved that Earth was not the only planet in the solar system.

   B. It proved that there were planets closer to the sun than Earth.

   C. It proved how accurate Galileo's telescope was.

   D. It helped prove that the sun was the center of our solar system.

> Think about the Galileo controversy.

17. What did the church believe at the time of Galileo?

   A. The sun was at the center of the solar system.

   B. The moon was at the center of the solar system.

   C. Earth was at the center of the solar system.

   D. The sun orbited the moon.

> Go back to review the paragraphs where this topic is discussed.

Test B   Name: _____

Galileo: Father of Modern Science *(cont.)*

18. What caused Galileo to be placed under house arrest?

    A. his theory that Earth was at the center of the solar system

    B. his theory that the sun was at the center of the solar system

    C. his discovery of Jupiter's moons

    D. his discovery of the phases of Venus

> Think about how Galileo's view conflicted with the church.

19. In what century did Galileo die?

    A. the 16th

    B. the 15th

    C. the 18th

    D. the 17th

> Think where the most likely place for this info would be.

20. Why was Galileo considered to be ahead of his time?

    A. He lived a long life.

    B. He believed his ideas would eventually be accepted based on his new discoveries.

    C. He made discoveries that would be important in the future.

    D. He invented new technology.

> Think about the meaning of the expression.

Type of Question: _____

Test B | Name: _____

Directions: Read the passage called "Homework or No Homework?: That Is the Question!" Then answer questions 21–30.

Homework or No Homework?: That Is the Question!

Over the past few years, there has been a lot of debate over something that has been a normal part of school for a long time. If you have gone to school in the United States then you have done this thing hundreds and hundreds of times. Homework!

But why is homework such an important part of school? For a long time, teachers and parents thought that homework helped students to learn the material that they needed to know. The idea is that if you are learning the times tables in school, you need to practice them at home so you will learn them faster. This seems to make sense and it is what most of us have done. Who hasn't sat at the kitchen table with a a stack of multiplication flash cards?

> What is the main idea of the passage?

But new research suggests that homework isn't as important as we once thought it was. This research is stirring up a lot of controversy because it proposes that the way we do homework should be radically changed.

Here are some of the reasons why homework has been thought to be an important part of a student's education:

- Homework keeps kids busy after school. If kids didn't have homework, they might have too much free time after school to get into trouble.

- Homework helps to reinforce the skills that students learn in school. You have to do a lot of practice to learn the content.

- Homework instills self discipline. Doing homework helps students learn the value of hard work.

> What is the author's opinion regarding the topic?

These are some of the ideas that people have had and that have remained unchanged for decades.

But new research suggests that homework doesn't help as much as we think it does. In fact, research suggests that homework might actually be harmful. Here is what some of the most recent research has discovered:

- Since 1981, the amount of time elementary students have spent on homework has increased by 51%.

- Elementary school students spend about 78 minutes a night doing homework.

- Doing 60 to 90 minutes of homework per night does not increase test scores of elementary school students.

Test B   Name: _____

Homework or No Homework?: That Is the Question! *(cont.)*

- Countries that have students who score well on tests, like Japan and Denmark, do not do homework.

- Too much homework decreases the amount of time that kids can spend outside being active.

- Too much homework can hurt a student's ability to learn because it makes learning less enjoyable.

So what should teachers do? Important people in the field say that instead of getting rid of homework, teachers should change the type of homework they give and how long it takes to do it. Here are a few guidelines that experts say might be helpful to students:

- Each grade level should only have 10 minutes of homework per night. First grade should have 10 minutes, second grade should have 20 minutes, etc.

- Homework should only be assigned Monday through Thursday.

- Homework should help develop study skills and good work habits.

- Homework should help students practice a skill.

- Homework should help students learn a bit more about something they already know.

Knowing what the research has discovered can help teachers to make decisions about the quality and quantity of the homework they expect their students to do each night. This in turn will help students master the skills they will need in order to achieve academic success.

Questions 21–30: Select the best answer.

21. What is the controversy in this passage that the author refers to?

   A. the importance of homework

   B. the importance of school

   C. school lunches

   D. how much time students should spend on homework

   > Think about what the debate is about.

22. According to the author, one of the reasons homework is valued is because

   A. it increases test scores.

   B. it actually makes kids smarter.

   C. it keeps kids busy and out of trouble.

   D. it is not done in Japan or Denmark.

   > Review the argument for homework.

Test B   Name: _____

Homework or No Homework?: That Is the Question! *(cont.)*

23. *Countries that have students who score well on tests, such as Japan and Denmark, do not do homework.* Identify the subject and predicate in this sentence.

    A. *high* and *students*

    B. *high test-scoring students* and *do not do homework*

    C. *Japan, Denmark* and *do not do*

    D. *countries* and *do not*

    > Remember, the subject is who or what the sentence is about.

24. What is the cause of changing attitudes about homework?

    A. Students have been complaining about how useless it is.

    B. Parents are tired of helping their kids do homework.

    C. Students keep getting low test scores.

    D. New research into the area.

    > Go back to this part of the passage.

25. What is the average time that an elementary school student spends on homework?

    A. 78 minutes

    B. 60 to 90 minutes

    C. 10 minutes

    D. 20 minutes

    > Point Right To It!

    Type of Question: _____

26. According to the guidelines, how much homework should a second grader receive on a Monday night?

    A. 20 minutes

    B. none

    C. 10 minutes

    D. 78 minutes

    > Read through all of the guidelines before you answer.

Test B   Name: _____

Homework or No Homework?: That Is the Question! *(cont.)*

27. According to the guidelines, how much homework should a sixth grader receive on a Monday night?

   A. 60 minutes

   B. 90 minutes

   C. 20 minutes

   D. 15 minutes

> Multiply to get the answer.

28. The research has found a connection between too much homework and

   A. overeating.

   B. school suspensions.

   C. bullying.

   D. lack of physical activity.

> Review the passage to find the answer.

29. How does the author support his or her case for less homework?

   A. The author uses bullet points.

   B. The author offers her opinion.

   C. The author is opposed to less homework.

   D. The author provides information about what recent research says.

> What is the author using to persuade the reader?

Type of Question: _____

30. According to the passage, which of the following would be an appropriate homework assignment?

   A. a research paper

   B. a few laps around the block

   C. adding and subtracting fractions

   D. reading for 90 minutes

> Make a deduction.

Test B   **Name:** _____

Directions: Read the poem called "The Last Leaf." Then answer questions 31–40.

The Last Leaf
by
Julia McMeans

Somewhere high up in a tree,
There is a leaf out on a branch,
A brown and dry and brittle thing,
Who'll soon be cast into the sea.

As he waits for certain fate,
He thinks of better days gone by,
When he was dewy, moist, and green,
And flit against a sky of slate.

One of thousands that was he,
An emerald peak, a rustling wave,
Which crested o'er the forest dense,
And shrouded woods in canopy.

Now the last of his great race,
He trembles like a frightened child,
And clings to the familiar branch,
To keep him in his usual place.

On his branch a bird alights,
And asks him, "Leaf, what do you fear?"
"What will become of me down there?
It seems a land of endless nights."

"Yes, I see your point of view,
But here you are a leaf alone.
With your brethren you will be,
When to this branch you bid adieu."

"Bird, I think you are quite wise;
The branches here have long been bare,
A single leaf cannot do much,
My fears I think I must revise."

> Identify the main character.

Test B   Name: _____

The Last Leaf *(cont.)*

Very soon the winter roared,
And bent the forest trees in half,
And rustled Leaf down to his stem,
Till from his branch he came unmoored.

Leaf was tussled, turned, and tossed,
He watched the swirling earth and sky,
Then smelled the salty mist below,
And landed in the sea quite lost.

Not for long for on a swell,
He spotted members of his kind,
A school of brown and brittle things,
That called him friend, he knew them well.

Leaf had learned that letting go,
Was really changing how you think,
And all the trepidation felt,
Are things of which you do not know.

Leaf and leaves on waves debate,
And talk of times on branches past,
When they were dewy, moist, and green,
While floating on a sea of slate.

> What is the poem's theme?

Questions 31–40: Select the best answer.

31. Who or what is the main character of this poem?

A. a leaf

B. a bird

C. a tree

D. the sea

> Use the process of elimination.

32. What words best describe the mood of the main character?

A. joyful and happy

B. courageous and sad

C. sad and fearful

D. confused and vain

> Think of the situation the leaf is in.

Test B Name: _____

The Last Leaf *(cont.)*

33. What does the leaf fear?

    A. birds

    B. squirrels

    C. falling off the tree

    D. the wind

> Look for what the leaf says.

34. What literary device does the author use?

    A. onomatopoeia

    B. simile

    C. irony

    D. personification

> Think of what each one of these describes.

35. What does "dewy, moist, and green" describe?

    A. the young leaf

    B. the old leaf

    C. the bird

    D. the sea

> Make an inference.

36. What perspective does the bird help the leaf to see?

    A. the bitterness of old age

    B. how pointless is it to hold on

    C. that if he falls he won't be alone anymore

    D. that birds use leaves to build nests

> Go back and find what the bird says.

37. What happens to the leaf when he first comes unmoored?

    A. He falls from the tree.

    B. He clings to the tree.

    C. He meets other leaves.

    D. He sleeps on the branch.

> Reread the stanza containing the word *unmoored* to determine the meaning.

Type of Question: _____

Test B Name: _____

The Last Leaf *(cont.)*

38. According to the poem, what do the sea and sky have in common?

    A. They are both feared by the leaf.

    B. They are both vast.

    C. They represent loneliness.

    (D.) They are both the same color.

> Look for adjectives that describe both things.

(39.) The description of the leaves as a school is an example of

    A. metaphor.

    B. pun.

    (C.) epigram.

    D. allusion.

> Connect the leaves and their location.

40. What is the theme of the poem?

    A. All things have a life cycle.

    (B.) Letting go of fear requires that you change how you think.

    C. All things suffer.

    D. Loneliness is sad.

> The theme is the message of the poem.

Type of Question: _____

| Test B | Name: _____ |

Directions: Read the retelling of the classic tale, "Cat and Mouse in Partnership." Then answer questions 41–50.

Cat and Mouse in Partnership
by
the Brothers Grimm

A cat made the acquaintance of a rather affable mouse, and had said so much to her, and flattered her with stories of great love, affection, and friendship that he felt for her, that at last the mouse agreed that they should live and keep house together.

> What type of story is this?

"But we must make preparations for the winter, or else we shall suffer from hunger, maybe even starvation," said the cat, "and you, little mouse, cannot venture out everywhere, or in the end you will be caught in a trap."

This excellent advice was followed, and they bought a pot of fat, but they did not know where to store it. Finally, after much pondering and consideration, the cat spoke.

"I know of no place where it will be better stored than in the church. No one would dare take anything from there. They'd be too intimidated. We'll put it beneath the altar, and not touch it until we are in desperate, dire need."

So the pot was stored safely away, but it was not long before the cat took a great longing for it, and said to the mouse, "I wanted to tell you, little mouse, that my cousin has brought a little son into the world, and she asked me to be his godfather. He is white with brown spots, and I am to hold him over the baptismal font. Let me go out today, and you look after the house by yourself."

"Yes, yes," squeaked the mouse. "By all means go, for you are obviously a venerated uncle, and if you get anything mouthwatering to eat, think of me. I would like to drink a drop of sweet, scrumptious, ruby-red christening wine myself."

All this, however, was untrue. A pure deceit on behalf of the cat, for he had no cousin at all, and had not been asked to be godfather. He went straight to the church, skulked up to the pot of fat, and began to lick at it feverishly, until he licked off the top layer of the fat. Then he went for a leisurely stroll on the roofs of the town, and then stretched out in the sun, licking his whiskers whenever he thought of the pot of fat. He did not return home until it was evening.

Test B   Name: _____

Cat and Mouse in Partnership (cont.)

"Well, I see you have returned," said the mouse. "You must have had a glorious day."

"Everything went superbly well," answered the cat. "I am highly esteemed by my kin."

"What name did they bestow on the child?" asked the mouse.

"Top-Off," said the cat quite indifferently.

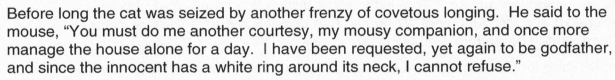

"Top-Off?" cried the mouse. "That is a very unconventional and uncommon name. Is it a common one in your family?"

"What possible difference does it make?" said the cat haughtily.

"It's no worse than Crumb-Thief, as your godchildren are called."

Before long the cat was seized by another frenzy of covetous longing. He said to the mouse, "You must do me another courtesy, my mousy companion, and once more manage the house alone for a day. I have been requested, yet again to be godfather, and since the innocent has a white ring around its neck, I cannot refuse."

The benevolent mouse consented. For being such a civil, courteous mouse, she did not want to prohibit the cat from performing his familial duty. For all she knew, the cat may have been the only uncle on which his family could depend. However, the cat, being the untrustworthy, duplicitous thing that he was, slinked silently behind the town wall to the church and devoured half of the vessel of fat.

"Nothing tastes as marvelous as that which one eats by oneself," he said, and was quite satisfied and enlivened with his day's labors.

> Think about the sequence of events in the story.

When he arrived home the mouse asked, "What name was this child christened with?"

"Half-Gone," responded the cat slyly.

"Half-Gone? How perplexing! You must have misspoke! I have never heard that name in all my life. I'll wager it is not on any list."

The cat's mouth soon again began to water for the savory and delicious delicacy. He could barely contain his fervor for the hidden refreshment and feared that his clandestine desire would soon become quite apparent to the mouse. She was gullible, but she wasn't blind!

"All good things come threefold," he said to the mouse. "I've been summoned a third time to be a godfather again. The child is totally black, as black as this kettle, as black as the night, the only white being his snowy alabaster paws. Otherwise, it has not a single white hair on its entire body. This is such an irregularity, such a rare occurrence, it happens only once every few years. You will permit me to go, won't you?"

"Top-Off. Half-Gone," answered the mouse. "These are such peculiar names, that they make me stop and think."

Test B	Name: _____

Cat and Mouse in Partnership (cont.)

"Here you sit at home," said the cat, "with your dark gray fur coat and long braid of hair inventing fantasies. That is because you don't go out during the daytime, and your feverish mousy mind turns to the world of phantoms and make-believe.

During the cat's absence, the mouse cleaned the house from top to bottom and arranged and organized every little thing, while the scheming avaricious feline devoured all of the rest of the fat. He didn't return home until nighttime.

The mouse immediately asked what name had been given to the third child.

"You will not like it either," said the cat suspiciously. "His name is All-Gone."

"All-Gone," cried the mouse. "That is the most disquieting name of all. I have never seen it in print. All-Gone! What can that possibly mean?" Then she shook her head, curled herself up, and lay down to sleep.

From this time forth no one invited the cat to be godfather, but when winter had arrived and there was no longer anything to be found outside, the mouse thought of their deposited food and said, "Come cat, we will go to our secret cache, our hidden stockpile of fat which we have wisely stored up for ourselves. It will taste absolutely scrumptious now, especially as there is nothing left outside to eat."

"Yes," answered the cat. "You will appreciate it as much as you would appreciate sticking that dainty, delicate tongue of yours out the window."

They set out on their journey, but when they arrived, the pot of fat, to be sure, was still in place, but it was completely empty. Not a single speck remained.

"Alas," said the mouse, "now I see what has happened. Now it comes to light! All of your deception is now revealed! You are a true friend," said mouse sarcastically. "You ate everything when you were serving as godfather. First Top-Off, then Half-Gone, then…"

> What has the mouse just figured out?

"Be quiet!" cried the cat. "One more word, and I'll eat you too."

"All-Gone" was already on the poor mouse's lips. She had scarcely spoken it before the cat sprang on her, seized her, and swallowed her down.

You see, that is the way of the world.

| Test B | Name: _____ |

Cat and Mouse in Partnership *(cont.)*

Questions 41–50: Select the best answer.

41. Why does the cat have to use flattery to get the mouse to live with him?

- **A.** Because the cat is a natural predator of the mouse.
- **B.** Because the cat really loves the mouse.
- **C.** Because the mouse is stubborn.
- **D.** Because it is in their best interests to live together.

Remember the types of questions that begin with why.

Type of Question: _____

42. Why is a church a good place to hide the fat?

- **A.** Because there are lots of good hiding places in churches.
- **B.** Because they are quiet and not many people go into them.
- **C.** Because people would feel especially bad about stealing from a church.
- **D.** Churches are typically very dark.

Make an inference.

43. What excuse does the cat keep giving to get away from the house?

- **A.** He says that it is only natural that a cat go out and hunt.
- **B.** He says that he has to visit his sick mother.
- **C.** He says that he has to go to work.
- **D.** He says that he has to visit his newly born nieces and nephews.

Go back and skim the passage to find the answer.

44. What is the best way to describe the names that the cat gives to his nephews?

- **A.** humorous
- **B.** sarcastic
- **C.** mean
- **D.** pretty

Use the process of elimination.

45. The fact that the animals in the story talk is an example of

- **A.** alliteration.
- **B.** denotation.
- **C.** hyperbole.
- **D.** personification.

Look for root words in the option for clues.

Test B   Name: _____

Cat and Mouse in Partnership *(cont.)*

46. What is the main relationship between the cat and mouse?

    A. The cat lies to the mouse, and the mouse believes everything he says.

    B. The mouse lies to the cat, and the cat is suspicious of everything that he says.

    C. The cat lies to the mouse, and the mouse doesn't believe a word of it.

    D. The mouse is tricking the cat into thinking she is not smart.

> Select the one that makes the most sense.

47. What does the cat accuse the mouse of having?

    A. a big belly

    B. a secret stash of fat

    C. his favorite toy

    D. an overactive imagination

> Find what the cat says to the mouse.

48. How does the name "All-Gone" foreshadow what is going to happen to the mouse?

    A. Because the fat is all gone.

    B. Because the cat eats the mouse.

    C. Because the mouse eats the cat.

    D. Because it is the end of the story.

> Refer to the end of the story.

49. How might you restate the last line of the story?

    A. Mice torment cats, and that's the way it is.

    B. The world is a dangerous place, so just accept it.

    C. The way of the world is to trust others.

    D. Cats eat mice, and that's the natural order of things.

> Reread the last line, and then say it in your own words.

50. Why is the title ironic?

    A. Because cats and mice are natural enemies.

    B. Because cats and mice are mammals.

    C. Because animals don't talk.

    D. Because animals don't live in houses.

> Reread the title.

| Test C | Name: _____ |

Directions: Read the passage called "How Silk Is Made." Then answer questions 1–10.

How Silk Is Made

Silk is one of the most sought-after materials in the world. It is used to make beautiful clothing. It is also used to weave intricate tapestries. Silk is a natural material. It is usually very expensive. One of the reasons silk is so costly is because of how complicated the silk-making process is.

Silk comes from a caterpillar called the *Bombyx mori*. This caterpillar is often called the silkworm or silkworm moth. The silkworm is blind and cannot fly. You may remember from science class that moths and butterflies undergo a four-step process of development:

First: The adult moth lays eggs.

Second: The eggs hatch and caterpillars (larvae) emerge.

Third: Each caterpillar pupates, or spins a cocoon, which is also called a *chrysalis*.

Fourth: The adult moth emerges from the cocoon.

The silkworm, however, does not get to complete this process of development. Its metamorphosis is interrupted. The flowchart on the next page explains how silkworms are cultivated in order to produce silk. This process is called *sericulture*. The production of silk is very labor intensive. It can take 2,500 cocoons to produce a single pound of silk.

The ancient Chinese were the first people to figure out how to cultivate the silkworm in order to produce silk. For thousands of years, they were the only people on Earth who knew how to do it. This secret of the Chinese helped to make silk one of the most sought after and traded materials in the ancient world. In fact, the Silk Road, one of the oldest trade routes, was named for this highly-prized fabric.

Test C   Name: _____

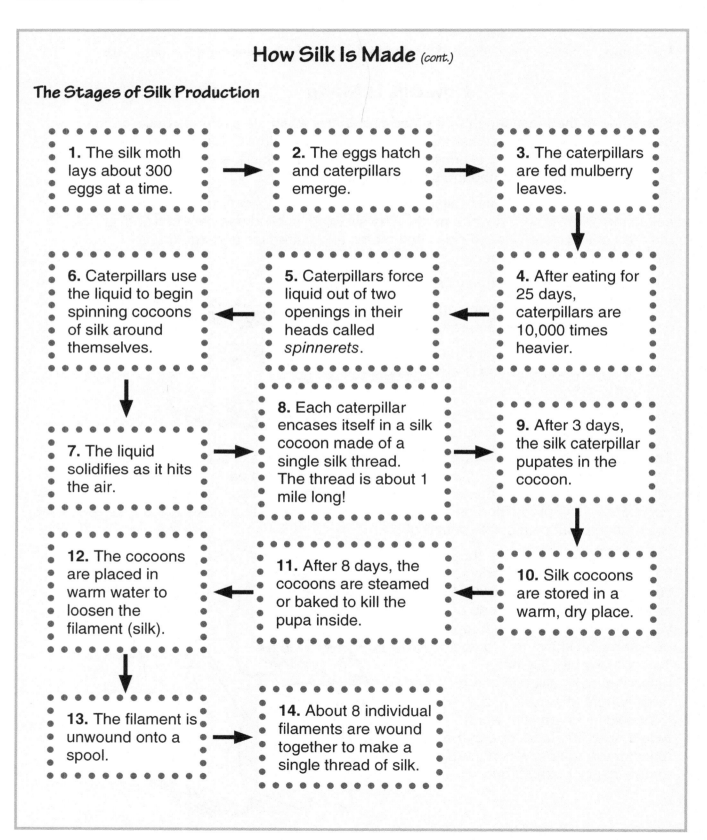

How Silk Is Made (cont.)

The Stages of Silk Production

1. The silk moth lays about 300 eggs at a time. → **2.** The eggs hatch and caterpillars emerge. → **3.** The caterpillars are fed mulberry leaves.

6. Caterpillars use the liquid to begin spinning cocoons of silk around themselves. ← **5.** Caterpillars force liquid out of two openings in their heads called *spinnerets*. ← **4.** After eating for 25 days, caterpillars are 10,000 times heavier.

7. The liquid solidifies as it hits the air. → **8.** Each caterpillar encases itself in a silk cocoon made of a single silk thread. The thread is about 1 mile long! → **9.** After 3 days, the silk caterpillar pupates in the cocoon.

12. The cocoons are placed in warm water to loosen the filament (silk). ← **11.** After 8 days, the cocoons are steamed or baked to kill the pupa inside. ← **10.** Silk cocoons are stored in a warm, dry place.

13. The filament is unwound onto a spool. → **14.** About 8 individual filaments are wound together to make a single thread of silk.

Test C | Name: _____

How Silk Is Made (cont.)

Questions 1–10: Select the best answer.

1. What is the official name of the silkworm?
   - **A.** silk moth
   - **B.** Chinese moth
   - **C.** *Bombyx*
   - **D.** *Bombyx mori*

2. Which of the following is *not* true about the silkworm?
   - **A.** The silkworm is blind.
   - **B.** The silkworm can fly.
   - **C.** The silkworm eats mulberry leaves.
   - **D.** The silkworm spins a cocoon.

3. What is another name for a chrysalis?
   - **A.** larva
   - **B.** egg
   - **C.** filament
   - **D.** cocoon

4. What is *sericulture*?
   - **A.** another name for the *Bobyx mori*
   - **B.** the ancient name for the Silk Road
   - **C.** a type of fabric
   - **D.** the cultivation of silkworms to produce silk

5. What does the word *metamorphosis* mean?
   - **A.** process of development
   - **B.** cocoon spinning
   - **C.** unwinding the filament
   - **D.** the hatching of the eggs

Test C   Name: _____

How Silk Is Made (cont.)

6. About how many eggs does the silk moth lay at one time?

   A. 300

   B. 25

   C. 2,500

   D. 10,000

7. What stage of silk production is described in step 13?

   A. The cocoons are placed in a warm, dry place.

   B. The liquid solidifies as it hits the air.

   C. The filament is unwound.

   D. The caterpillars are fed mulberry leaves.

8. In which step of the silk-making process are the pupa killed?

   A. 10

   B. 11

   C. 1

   D. the last step

9. Which of the following is the best estimate for how long it might take to make a single thread of silk?

   A. 25 days

   B. 8 days

   C. 3 days

   D. 36 days

10. How do you think silk production affected the ancient Chinese?

   A. It probably made them powerful.

   B. It probably made them weak.

   C. It probably created many famines.

   D. It would have had no effect as they were the only ones who knew how to make silk.

Test C   Name: _____

Directions: Read the passage called "Thanking the Animals." Then answer questions 11–20.

Thanking the Animals

Do you live with a cat or a dog? If you do, then you are one of many Americans who do. There are millions of people in the United States who live with dogs, cats, fish, hamsters, and even snakes! Animals that live with people as friends are called pets. But if you look a little closer, you will see another kind of connection between people and animals. It is based on a process called *domestication*.

Food, Clothing, and Medicine

Domestication means to tame and control animals to meet basic human needs. Some of these animals are used to feed people. People eat beef, pork, and eggs, which come from cows, pigs, and chickens. Most Americans also enjoy dairy products. Dairy products like milk, cheese, and yogurt also come from animals. Animals that are used as food are called *livestock*.

The skin and fur of animals are used to make clothing. Leather, wool, and silk come from animals. People have used the hides of animals to build shelters. Animal bones and horns have been carved into tools and weapons.

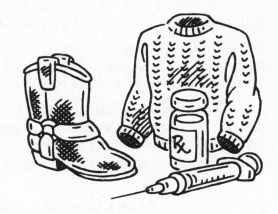

Different parts of animals are used to make many of the medicines that we use every day. Insulin, which is used for the treatment of diabetes, once came from animals.

People have used animals to help them do work for thousands of years. Horses and camels have been used to transport people and goods. Certain breeds of dogs herd sheep and goats. In the past, oxen pulled the plows that tilled the fields. Donkeys and elephants were used to carry heavy loads, and horses were used in warfare.

You can see animals hard at work today. They pull carriages around landscaped parks and help people with such disabilities as blindness to get around safely.

Test C — Name: _____

Thanking the Animals *(cont.)*

Guidelines for Domestication

Not every type of animal can be domesticated. Some animals are too scared of people. Others may be too aggressive. Here are some of the rules that determine whether an animal can be domesticated or not:

- **Flexible Diet:** A flexible diet means that the animals can eat lots of different things. For example, horses can eat grass, oats, apples, and carrots! It's also good if the animal doesn't eat many of the same things people eat. That might create competition.

- **Fast Growers:** The animal must reach adulthood quickly. The faster the animal grows up, the sooner it can produce milk or herd sheep.

- **Captive Breeding:** The animal must be able to breed in captivity. This means that it can produce offspring without too much trouble. Some animals have a hard time doing this if they are around people or are contained in a cage or other enclosure.

- **Friendly:** The animal has to have a pleasant personality or like to be around people. If an animal is too aggressive, it might be a danger to people.

- **Calm:** The animal should have a fairly calm disposition. It wouldn't be good for people or the animal if it were always frightened and likely to run away if it felt trapped.

- **Respects the Boss:** There are some types of animals that live in social groups that have leaders and followers. These kinds of animals are good candidates for domestication because they will recognize the human as being in charge.

Human beings have domesticated animals for over 10,000 years. These animals help us meet our basic needs and enrich our lives. The work that animals do for us can be hard and scary. Often, animals lose their lives so that our lives can be better and easier. Animals make a huge contribution to people. So the next time you see a horse, a chicken, or a fish, say thank you!

Animal Domestication Timeline

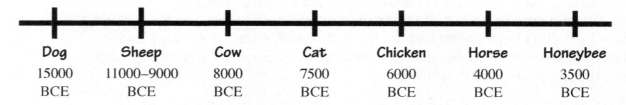

Dog	Sheep	Cow	Cat	Chicken	Horse	Honeybee
15000 BCE	11000–9000 BCE	8000 BCE	7500 BCE	6000 BCE	4000 BCE	3500 BCE

★ Dates are approximate.

Test C   Name: _____

Thanking the Animals *(cont.)*

Questions: 11–20: Select the best answer.

11. What is domestication?

  A. turning an animal into a pet

  B. taming animals to meet basic needs

  C. using bones to make tools

  D. using animals to do medical research

12. Which animal is an example of livestock?

  A. tiger

  B. mule

  C. sheep

  D. dog

13. Which of the following is *not* an example of how animals help people?

  A. a dog sniffing for bombs

  B. a bear performing in the circus

  C. a dog herding sheep

  D. a sheep providing wool

14. Which of the following is an example of a flexible diet?

  A. an animal that can eat fruit, leaves, and insects

  B. an animal that eats grass

  C. an animal that eats meat

  D. an animal that eats worms

15. Why can't some animals breed in captivity?

  A. They resent the presence of humans.

  B. They are too aggressive.

  C. They don't have a flexible diet.

  D. They don't like being contained in an enclosure.

| Test C | Name: _____ |

Thanking the Animals *(cont.)*

16. Which of the following would be the best candidate for domestication?

    A. an animal that reaches adulthood in 18 months

    B. an animal that reaches adulthood in 20 months

    C. an animal that reaches adulthood in 11 months

    D. an animal that reaches adulthood in 12 months

17. According to the timeline, which animal was domesticated first?

    A. horse

    B. dog

    C. honeybee

    D. cow

18. The camel was domesticated in 2500 BCE. Where would that go on the timeline?

    A. before the sheep

    B. after the honeybee

    C. before the cat

    D. in between the cow and the cat

19. The author states that "animals make a huge contribution to people." What is this statement based on?

    A. facts based on evidence and examples provided

    B. the author's personal opinion

    C. the author's love of animals

    D. the importance of pets

20. How do you think the author feels about domesticated animals?

    A. greedy

    B. kind

    C. resentful

    D. grateful

Test C   Name: _____

Directions: Read the passage called "A Woman's Right to Vote." Then answer questions 21–30.

A Woman's Right to Vote

In the United States everyone who is 18 years old has suffrage. *Suffrage* means that you have the right to vote in elections and run for office. But there was a time in our history when many different groups of people did not have these rights. The right to vote was something for which people had to fight.

The last group of people in our country who couldn't vote was women. But things started to change in the 19th century. Women sought equal rights with men. They protested to end discrimination. *Discrimination* means to keep one group of people from doing something that another group of people can do because of race, gender, or religion. Women were discriminated against just because they were women. One of the main things women wanted was suffrage. They knew that if they could vote, then they would have a say in how the country was governed.

In 1848, Elizabeth Cady Stanton and Lucretia Mott held a conference to talk about the issues that affected women. This meeting was held in Seneca Falls, New York. One of the main topics was voting rights. They said that a woman's right to vote was sacred. That means that the right to vote was not something that one group of people could deny another group. It was a God-given right.

Susan B. Anthony, Elizabeth Cady Stanton, and Lucy Stone became leaders of the Women's Rights Movement in the 1850s. They worked hard to pressure state legislatures to grant women suffrage. But in the 1860s, the Civil War began. During this time, the women stopped their protests for the voting rights. Instead, many in this movement worked to help free slaves in the United States.

In the 1890s, two different women's rights groups merged. They became the National American Woman's Suffrage Association (NAWSA). Carrie Chapman was the group's leader. She started a campaign to win women the right to vote. She got the support of women who had wealth and power. They had parades and demonstrations. In 1920, the 19th amendment, granting women suffrage, was ratified. It had been 72 years since the convention in Seneca Falls, but finally women had won the right to vote.

Women's suffrage was a worldwide movement. There were many countries that denied women the right to vote. Stanton and Anthony founded the International Council for Women. This group worked to help women in other parts of the world get the right to vote.

Test C   Name: _____

A Woman's Right to Vote *(cont.)*

They also fought for other women's issues, such as equal pay for equal work and the right to an education.

Many different women throughout the 20th century have had to fight for the same rights as men. But it all started in the 19th century with Stanton, Anthony, and Stone. In 2012, there were almost 100 women serving in the United States Congress and six women who governed states. In the presidential election of 2008, 66% of the people who voted were women.

Questions: 21–30: Select the best answer.

21. What is suffrage?

    A. the right to vote

    B. the right to run for elected office

    C. the right to equal pay

    D. the right to vote and run for elected office

22. How old do you have to be in the United States to vote?

    A. 21

    B. 18

    C. 25

    D. 16

23. When did the women's suffrage movement begin?

    A. the 1900s

    B. the 1800s

    C. 1920

    D. 1776

24. What is the significance of Seneca Falls?

    A. It is the location of the first battle of the Civil War.

    B. It is the birthplace of Elizabeth Cady Stanton.

    C. It is the location of an important women's rights conference.

    D. It is where the 19th amendment was signed into law.

Test C	Name: _____

A Woman's Right to Vote (cont.)

25. Which of the following is *not* an example of discrimination?

    A. a 10-year-old child not being allowed to drive

    B. an African American not being allowed to attend the school of their choice

    C. a woman not being able to join a club or group

    D. These are all examples of discrimination.

26. Why did the Women's Rights Movement stop protesting during the Civil War?

    A. The movement was made illegal.

    B. Women stopped caring about the right to vote.

    C. They focused their efforts on freeing slaves.

    D. It was considered rude to protest during a time of war.

27. What is the NAWSA?

    A. National American Woman's Suffrage Association

    B. National Association of Women's Suffrage of America

    C. National American Women's Movement

    D. National Women's Suffrage Movement

28. What amendment guarantees suffrage to women?

    A. 20th

    B. 15th

    C. 21st

    D. 19th

29. In what year were women granted the right to vote?

    A. 1920

    B. 1848

    C. 1890

    D. 1800

30. In 2012, about how many women served in the United States Congress?

    A. 6

    B. 66

    C. 10

    D. about 100

Test C   Name: _____

Directions: Read the passage called "Equal Pay for Equal Work." Then answer questions 31–40.

Equal Pay for Equal Work

Women in the Workforce

Women in the United States have always had to fight for their rights. In the 19th century, the suffragettes fought to win women the right to vote and run for elected office. One area in which women have had a long struggle is in the workplace. Women have often been paid unfairly in their jobs. Sometimes, women get paid less money for doing the same job as men.

Before World War II, most women worked in the home. But once the war started, millions of American men went off to fight. The jobs that the men once had were vacated. For this reason, many women entered the workforce. They worked in factories and offices.

Unfortunately, many of the companies that hired women only offered them low-paying jobs. Newspapers published separate job listings for men and women. And in the 1950s, women were paid almost half of what men earned.

In 1963, the Equal Pay Act was signed by President Kennedy. An act is a new law. This act made it illegal to pay women less than men for doing the same job. This act helped narrow the income gap between the sexes, but there were still battles to be fought and won.

Lilly Ledbetter

In 2009, the Lilly Ledbetter Fair Pay Act was passed. This new law was named after Lilly Ledbetter. Because of what Lilly Ledbetter did, women have a better chance of being paid fairly at work. The new law makes it harder for employers to discriminate against a person because she is a woman.

In 1998, Ledbetter was going to retire. She worked at Goodyear Tire and Rubber Company. She worked there for 19 years. The whole time that she worked there she didn't know that the men in the company were getting paid more than she was even though they were doing the same work. Mrs. Ledbetter earned $3,727 per month. The men that she worked with earned between $4,286 and $5,236 a month. That's a difference of about $1,500 per month!

Once Ledbetter found out, she filled a lawsuit against Goodyear. In her suit, she said that the company was paying her less just because she was a woman. A jury ruled in her favor. And Ledbetter won the case. But in 2007, the Supreme Court overturned this decision.

Test C   Name: _____

Equal Pay for Equal Work *(cont.)*

Lilly Ledbetter *(cont.)*

They said that she waited too long to file a complaint against Goodyear. The Supreme Court said that she should have filed a complaint within 180 days of her first unequal paycheck. But there was no way that Ledbetter could have done that. She did not know that she was being paid unfairly. Most companies keep information about salaries private.

Ledbetter Fights Back

Ledbetter petitioned the Congress to write a new law, one that made it easier for people to sue for equal pay. It took her over two years, but her persistence paid off. In 2009, President Obama signed the Lilly Ledbetter Fair Pay Act. It was the first law that he signed as president. The new law states that people can file a complaint about unfair pay within 180 days of their most recent paycheck, not their first paycheck. When President Obama signed the Lilly Ledbetter Fair Pay Act, he said:

"Today, I signed this bill, not just in Lilly's honor, but for my daughters and all those who will come after us. I want them to grow up in a nation where there are no limits to their dreams."

Questions 31–40: Select the best answer.

31. Which of the following tells the main idea of the first paragraph?

    A. Women have always suffered discrimination.

    B. Workplace rules are often unfair.

    C. Women have had to fight for equal pay.

    D. The suffragettes had to fight to get the right to vote.

32. What caused so many women to enter the workforce?

    A. World War I

    B. World War II

    C. suffrage

    D. the Lilly Ledbetter Fair Pay Act

Test C   **Name:** _____

Equal Pay for Equal Work *(cont.)*

33. What does the term *income gap* mean in this passage?

   A. It is the difference in income between high and low paying jobs.

   B. It is the difference in income between factory and office jobs.

   C. It is the difference between Ledbetter's salary and that of the men at Goodyear.

   D. It is the difference in income between what men and women earn.

34. Which president signed the Equal Pay Act into law?

   A. President Obama

   B. President Bush

   C. President Kennedy

   D. President Clinton

35. Why did Lilly Ledbetter sue Goodyear?

   A. because the men doing the same work were being paid more

   B. because she was forced to work longer hours than the men

   C. because the men were being paid less than she was

   D. because she was forced to retire before she wanted to

36. Why did the Supreme Court overturn Ledbetter's case?

   A. There was no proof of sexual discrimination.

   B. They said Ledbetter waited too long to file a complaint.

   C. They said she filed a complaint too soon.

   D. Coworkers testified that Ledbetter was not a hard worker.

37. What prevented Ledbetter from filing a complaint sooner than she did?

   A. She kept putting it off.

   B. Goodyear told her that they would take care of the problem.

   C. She had no idea that she was being discriminated against.

   D. She couldn't find a lawyer who would take up her case.

Test C   Name: _____

Equal Pay for Equal Work *(cont.)*

38. What does the Lilly Ledbetter Fair Pay Act say about when a person can file a complaint?

    A. You can file a complaint within 180 days of your first paycheck.

    B. You can file a complaint within the first 180 days of your employment at a company.

    C. You can file a complaint at anytime.

    D. You can file a complaint within 180 days of your most recent paycheck.

39. In what year was the Lilly Ledbetter Fair Pay Act signed into law?

    A. 2009

    B. 1963

    C. during World War II

    D. 2012

40. Why do you think President Obama mentions his daughters when he signed the Lilly Ledbetter Fair Pay Act?

    A. He loves his daughters.

    B. He thinks of Lilly Ledbetter as a daughter.

    C. Because the Lilly Ledbetter Fair Pay Act will affect his daughters.

    D. Because his daughters supported the Lilly Ledbetter Fair Pay Act.

Test C   Name: _____

Directions: Read the story "Say Cheese." Then answer questions 41–50.

Say Cheese

Parmesan on Fridays

Every day on my way home from school, I walk past Say Cheese. Say Cheese is an amazing cheese shop right in my neighborhood, Tecumseh Springs. Tecumseh is the name of a famous Native American who used to live here centuries ago.

Say Cheese is owned by Mr. Folietti. Everyone calls him Foli for short. On Fridays, I stop by the shop to say hello to Foli. As soon as you walk into Say Cheese you are overcome with the smell of hundreds of different cheeses. It's impossible to go in there without your mouth starting to water.

Foli sells plenty of cheeses that people eat every day, such as Cheddar, Swiss, and Limburger. But then he has all these other kinds of cheeses from all over the world that I'd never heard of before. For instance, at Say Cheese, you can get Camembert cheese from France, which is really soft and easy to spread. There is Blue Wensleydale from England and even Bundz cheese from Poland. Foli has cheese that is made from the milk of cows, sheep, goats, and buffalos. Out of all of the cheeses he has, my favorite is Parmesan-Reggiano. Parmesan is made in Italy. It is salty and delicious.

"Hey there, Keyshawn," Foli said as I walked into the shop. As soon as Foli sees me he shaves off a piece of Parmesan cheese from a giant wheel. He puts it in a little piece of wax paper and hands it to me.

"Wow, I think I could eat that whole wheel! Thanks, Foli."

All of the walls inside of Say Cheese are made of red bricks that have been painted white. On one of these white brick walls there is a large painting of some kind of a fish. I figured the paint was old because it was faded, cracked, and missing in some places.

"Hey Foli, why is there a picture of a big fish on your wall if this is a cheese shop? Shouldn't you have a cow or something like that?"

"Well, long before this was a cheese shop it was a fishmonger's shop."

"A fish what?" I asked. I had never heard of that before.

"A fishmonger," Foli said, "is a person who sells fish."

Foli explained that back in the day, before grocery stores, people got their goods from different shops that would all be lined up on the main street. You got your meat from a butcher, your fruit and vegetables from a greengrocer, and your fish from a fishmonger.

Test C   Name: _____

Say Cheese *(cont.)*

Parmesan on Fridays *(cont.)*

I found out that Foli's father bought the building from the fishmonger in 1932, over 80 years ago.

"But the building is nearly 200 years old," Foli said. "Sometimes I wonder what it was before it was a fishmonger's."

Foli shaved off another piece of Parmesan for me.

"I have an idea, Keyshawn, why don't you Google it? Find out what this place was before it was a fishmonger's."

The Library Time Machine

So I did. But I couldn't find what I was looking for online. My teacher, Mr. Lee, suggested that I do it the old fashioned way by going to the local library.

Tecumseh Springs has its own local branch of the library, and soon I found out that they had a collection of really old newspapers and photographs of how the main street looked, 50, 60, and even a 100 years ago.

Mrs. Elliot set me up at a table in the back of the library and gave me a whole bunch of data to look through. Fortunately, a lot of the old photos had been scanned into the computer, so I did more clicking than page turning.

Looking through all of the old photos of Tecumseh Springs was like being in a time machine. The most recent ones looked familiar, the store, the street signs, even the size of the trees. But the older the photos got, the more alien Tecumseh Springs began to look to me. In one of the photos, the old oak tree that stands at the corner of Cherokee and Summit was just a sapling, and the road went from paved, to cobblestone, to nothing but dirt!

Then, suddenly I saw it, a photo of Cohen's Fishmongers right there where Say Cheese stands today! In the picture there is a man standing outside of the shop, holding some kind of big dead fish by the tail.

So Say Cheese was once called Cohen's Fishmongers, but what was it before that? Back I went in time, until I found another old photo, dated 1877, of a shop called Mission Millinery.

"Mission Millinery" I said to myself. "What is millinery?"

I Googled it and my first search result was from Wikipedia. According to them, *millinery* is the designing and manufacture of ladies' hats.

So Mission Millinery became Cohen's Fishmongers, which in turn became Say Cheese. I couldn't wait to tell Foli that he was selling cheese in a former hat store!

Test C   Name: _____

Say Cheese (cont.)

Time Links

"Are you serious?" Foli asked, as he shaved me a slice of Parmesan.

"Yup! Here, take a look at the photos."

I had made several copies of the photos to bring to Foli. I had the picture of the fishmonger in the white apron, and another photo of a fancy hat with feathers and ribbons in the window of Mission Millinery.

"Incredible," Foli said. "Hey, I have an idea."

Foli went to the back of his store and then returned with two picture frames.

"Let's frame these and hang them on the wall with the giant painted fish."

As we were working on hanging the pictures, I asked, "Foli, 100 years from now, what do you think Say Cheese will be?"

"Good question," Foli said, as he mounted one of the pictures on the wall.

"Now I have an idea," I said.

Foli and I went outside of Say Cheese. We asked Mary Anne, the lady who runs the coffee shop next door, to come and take a picture of Foli and me standing in front of the store.

"Make sure you get the Say Cheese sign in the picture," Foli said.

Mary Anne focused her camera and then said, "Say cheese!"

Foli and I cracked up. We made a copy of the photo, framed it, and hung it with the pictures of Mission Millinery and Cohen's Fishmongers, right next to the big painted fish.

Questions 41–50: Select the best answer.

41. What is the name of the main character in the story?

    A. Mr. Folietti

    B. Keyshawn

    C. Mary Anne

    D. Mr. Lee

42. Why is Say Cheese a good name for a cheese shop?

    A. Because the product the store sells is in the name of the store.

    B. Because it is a play on words and names the word of the product it sells.

    C. It is short.

    D. It is easy to spell.

Test C   Name: _____

Say Cheese *(cont.)*

43. Where is Keyshawn's favorite cheese from?

    A. England

    B. France

    C. Poland

    (D.) Italy

44. Who bought the building from Cohen?

    (A.) Foli

    B. Mission Millinery

    (C.) Foli's father

    D. the candlestick maker

45. Why does Keyshawn feel like he is in a time machine?

    A. Because he just watched a movie about time travel.

    (B.) Because he is looking at photos from a long time ago.

    C. The old photo room in the library is called the time machine.

    D. Keyshawn is in a time machine.

46. What did the earliest roads in Tecumseh Springs look like?

    A. paved

    B. cobblestone

    C. bumpy

    (D.) dirt

47. What is a milliner?

    A. a person who sells fish

    (B.) a person who designs ladies' hats

    C. a greengrocer

    D. a cobbler

Test C Name: _____

Say Cheese *(cont.)*

48. What is Foli teaching Keyshawn by hanging the old photos in his shop?

    A. good business skills

    B. how to decorate a store

    C. respect for people of the past

    D. all of these

49. What is Keyshawn's idea?

    A. to get a picture of himself and Foli outside of the cheese shop

    B. to do research in the library about the past

    C. to be open-minded about trying different cheeses

    D. to become a milliner

50. Why is the last section of the story called "Time Links"?

    A. This section is about researching the past.

    B. This section is about researching the future.

    C. This section is about how the past, present, and future are connected.

    D. Because it comes after the "Library Time Machine" section.

Name: _____ **Date:** _____

Bubble Answer Sheet   Test _____

1. (A) (B) (C) (D)   18. (A) (B) (C) (D)   35. (A) (B) (C) (D)

2. (A) (B) (C) (D)   19. (A) (B) (C) (D)   36. (A) (B) (C) (D)

3. (A) (B) (C) (D)   20. (A) (B) (C) (D)   37. (A) (B) (C) (D)

4. (A) (B) (C) (D)   21. (A) (B) (C) (D)   38. (A) (B) (C) (D)

5. (A) (B) (C) (D)   22. (A) (B) (C) (D)   39. (A) (B) (C) (D)

6. (A) (B) (C) (D)   23. (A) (B) (C) (D)   40. (A) (B) (C) (D)

7. (A) (B) (C) (D)   24. (A) (B) (C) (D)   41. (A) (B) (C) (D)

8. (A) (B) (C) (D)   25. (A) (B) (C) (D)   42. (A) (B) (C) (D)

9. (A) (B) (C) (D)   26. (A) (B) (C) (D)   43. (A) (B) (C) (D)

10. (A) (B) (C) (D)   27. (A) (B) (C) (D)   44. (A) (B) (C) (D)

11. (A) (B) (C) (D)   28. (A) (B) (C) (D)   45. (A) (B) (C) (D)

12. (A) (B) (C) (D)   29. (A) (B) (C) (D)   46. (A) (B) (C) (D)

13. (A) (B) (C) (D)   30. (A) (B) (C) (D)   47. (A) (B) (C) (D)

14. (A) (B) (C) (D)   31. (A) (B) (C) (D)   48. (A) (B) (C) (D)

15. (A) (B) (C) (D)   32. (A) (B) (C) (D)   49. (A) (B) (C) (D)

16. (A) (B) (C) (D)   33. (A) (B) (C) (D)   50. (A) (B) (C) (D)

17. (A) (B) (C) (D)   34. (A) (B) (C) (D)

Master Answer Sheet for Tests A, B, and C

Answers for Test A (pages 18–39)

1. A	6. C	11. B	16. C	21. B	26. D	31. D.	36. A	41. C	46. B
2. C	7. A	12. D	17. A	22. B	27. A	32. A	37. B	42. B	47. C
3. D	8. B	13. B	18. D	23. C	28. C	33. B	38. C	43. D	48. D
4. C	9. A	14. A	19. B	24. C	29. A	34. A	39. D	44. C	49. A
5. A	10. B	15. B	20. C	25. C	30. C	35. C	40. D	45. B	50. A

Answers for Test B (pages 40–62)

1. C	6. B	11. C	16. D	21. A	26. A	31. A	36. C	41. A	46. A
2. D	7. D	12. B	17. C	22. C	27. A	32. C	37. A	42. C	47. D
3 B	8. A	13. B	18. B	23. B	28. D	33. C	38. D	43. D	48. B
4. D	9. C	14. A	19. D	24. D	29. D	34. D	39. A	44. B	49. D
5. A	10. D	15. A	20. C	25. A	30. C	35. A	40. B	45. D	50. A

Answers for Test C (pages 63–82)

1. D	6. A	11. B	16. C	21. D	26. C	31. C	36. B	41. B	46. D
2. B	7. C	12. C	17. B	22. B	27. A	32. B	37. C	42. B	47. B
3. D	8. B	13. B	18. B	23. B	28. D	33. D	38. D	43. D	48. C
4. D	9. D	14. A	19. A	24. C	29. A	34. C	39. A	44. C	49. A
5. A	10. A	15. D	20. D	25. A	30. D	35. A	40. C	45. B	50. C

Test A Answer Key

1. A	6. C	11.B	16.C	21.B	26.D	31.D.	36.A	41.C	46.B
2. C	7. A	12.D	17.A	22.B	27.A	32.A	37.B	42.B	47.C
3. D	8. B	13.B	18.D	23.C	28.C	33.B	38.C	43.D	48.D
4. C	9. A	14.A	19.B	24.C	29.A	34.A	39.D	44.C	49.A
5. A	10.B	15.B	20.C	25.C	30.C	35.C	40.D	45.B	50.A

Explanations for Test A Answers
Ancient Egyptian Mummification (pages 18–21)

1. **Correct Answer: A** *(Vocabulary)*
   Intentionally means to do something on purpose.
   Incorrect Answers:
   B. *Accidentally* is the opposite of intentionally.
   C. *Deceased* means dead.
   D. There is no single word that means *wrapped in linen*.

2. **Correct Answer: C** *(Determining Meaning: Prefixes)* I
   The passage states that *embalm* means to inject chemicals into the body to preserve it.
   Incorrect Answers:
   A. The prefix *ex* means *out of*.
   B. There is no mention of the veins in the passage.
   D. The prefix *meso* means *between*.

3. **Correct Answer: D** *(Locating Details)*
   The passage clearly states that what happens to the body at the point of death is connected to religious belief.
   Incorrect Answers:
   A. How old a person is when they die does not determine what happens to the body after death.
   B. Where a person is when they die does not affect what happens to the body.
   C. The *ba* and the *ka* are only connected to ancient Egyptian burial practices.

4. **Correct Answer: C** *(Locating Details)*
   The author states that the *ba* is similar to the idea of a conscience or personality.
   Incorrect Answers:
   A. The passage talks about the *ka*, or life force, and states that, when combined with the ba, it is like the soul.
   B. The *ka* is the life-force.
   D. Mohammad is mentioned in the passage, but he is not compared to the *ba*.

5. **Correct Answer: A** *(Locating Details)* E
   The passage clearly states that the *ka* needs food and drink in order to join the gods.
   Incorrect Answers:
   B. The *ba* needs the mummy, not the food and drink.
   C. The ancient Egyptian gods don't need to be appeased with food and drink.
   D. The mummy is a dead person and was not considered to be alive by the ancient Egyptians.

6. **Correct Answer: C** *(Locating Details)* E
   The passage states that the *ba* goes to be with the gods during the day.
   Incorrect Answers:
   A. The *ba* leaves the mummy during the day.
   B. The *ba* goes to be with the *ka*, who is already with the gods.
   D. The *ba* rests inside of the mummy at night, not beside it during the day.

7. **Correct Answer: A** *(Making Deductions)* I
   The *ba* travels back and forth between the mummy and the gods, so wings would allow it to do that.
   Incorrect Answers:
   B. There is no mention of feathers used for any purpose.
   C. Birds are not inserted inside of the mummy.
   D. The ancient Egyptians did worship birds, but that is not covered in this passage.

8. **Correct Answer: B** *(Locating Details)*
   The passage states that the *ba* needed a place to return to at night, and this is the purpose of the mummy.
   Incorrect Answers:
   A. Mummification was not experimental.
   C. The *ka* joined the gods. It had no other purpose than that.
   D. Generally, this may be true, but the most specific answer is B.

9. **Correct Answer: A** *(Making Deductions)*
   The opposite of mummification, or the intentional preservation of a corpse, would be cremation, which is the destruction of the corpse by burning.
   Incorrect Answers:
   B. *Entombment* means to bury, which is not the opposite of mummification.
   C. Mummification involved embalming, so this is not the opposite of the process.
   D. To deface the body would mean to spoil its appearance, but not destroy the body altogether.

10. **Correct Answer: B** *(Identifying Main Idea, Inferred)* E
    The passage explains mummification in the context of ancient Egyptian religious beliefs and practices.
    Incorrect Answers:
    A. Mummification is not a celebration.
    C. Mummification is not a political act.
    D. Mummification is not an act of rebellion.

Explanations for Test A Answers *(cont.)*

How to Make a Mummy *(pages 22–25)*

11. Correct Answer: B *(Locating Details)* **E**
The passage states that embalmers performed mummification.
Incorrect Answers:
- **A.** Priests do not perform the mummification process.
- **C.** Horus is the ancient Egyptian god of the afterlife, but he does not perform the mummification process.
- **D.** Mummy doctor is an invented term.

12. Correct Answers: D *(Determining Meaning, Context Clues)* **I**
The passage states that the organs are removed through the incision.
Incorrect Answers:
- **A.** An incision is not a synonym for a mummy.
- **B.** Natron is a type of preserving salt, not an incision.
- **C.** The abdomen is cut, but it is not the incision.

13. Correct Answer: B *(Making Deductions)* **I**
The brain is encased in a hard skull, so you can deduce that it can't be removed through an incision.
Incorrect Answers:
- **A.** The brain was not preserved.
- **C.** The embalmers did not drink the liquefied brain.
- **D.** Option B is correct so option D must be incorrect.

14. Correct Answer: A *(Making Deductions)* **I**
You can deduce that the organs the ancient Egyptians saved were valued, and those they discarded were not.
Incorrect Answers:
- **B.** If the ancient Egyptians wanted to preserve the brain, they could have made a canopic jar large enough to hold it.
- **C.** The ancient Egyptians did know how to store liquids.
- **D.** The brain was discarded. It was *not* considered sacred.

15. Correct Answer: B *(Making Inferences)*
The passage states that a special amulet is placed over the heart, the implication being that the heart is not removed.
Incorrect Answers:
- **A.** The stomach is removed.
- **C.** The liver is removed.
- **D.** The lungs are removed.

16. Correct Answer: C *(Locating Details)* **E**
Step 13 states that a Wadjet eye is placed over the incision.
Incorrect Answers:
- **A.** Other types of amulets are placed between the linens.
- **B.** A mask is placed over the face, but nothing is placed beneath it.
- **D.** Technically, the Wadjet eye is placed in the sarcophagus because the entire mummy is placed in there, but option C is more specific.

17. Correct Answer: A *(Making Deductions)*
Step 8, drying out the corpse, takes 40 days. No other step here would take that long.
Incorrect Answers:
- **B.** Step 22 is placing the sarcophagus into a tomb, something that would not take 40 days.
- **C.** Step 3 is removing the organs, which would not take 40 days.
- **D.** Step 4 is removing the brain. This would not take 40 days.

18. Correct Answer: D *(Locating Details)* **E**
Step 12 explicitly states that the body is brushed with pine resin to seal it.

Incorrect Answers:
- **A.** Natron, not pine resin, is used to dry out the body.
- **B.** Oil, not pine resin, is used to scent the body.
- **C.** A label is used to identify the body, not pine resin.

19. Correct Answer: B *(Sequencing)*
Wrapping the body in linen is step 15. The preceding step, 14, is the purification of the air.
Incorrect Answers:
- **A.** Step 13 involves the Wadjet eye.
- **C.** Step 17 involves the vulture amulet.
- **D.** The body is covered in natron, not brushed with it. Natron is involved in step 7.

20. Correct Answer: C *(Making Inferences)* **I**
A sarcophagus is something in which a body is placed and buried. You can infer that this is very much like a modern-day coffin.
Incorrect Answers:
- **A.** A mausoleum is an above ground room in which the dead are entombed.
- **B.** A pyramid is akin to a cemetery.
- **D.** Linen is the cloth a corpse is wrapped in, not the container in which it is buried.

Casey at the Bat *(pages 26–29)*

21. Correct Answer: B *(Interpreting Poetry, Rhyme Scheme)*
The rhyme scheme *aabb* means that lines 1 and 2 rhyme, and lines 3 and 4 rhyme in the stanza.
Incorrect Answers:
- **A.** *abab* would mean that the first and third lines rhyme and the second and fourth lines rhyme.
- **C.** *abca* would mean that the first and fourth lines in the stanza rhyme, and the second and third do not rhyme.
- **D.** *baba* is not a rhyme scheme.

22. Correct Answer: B *(Drawing Conclusions)*
The poem makes many references to a game played with bats, balls, and nine players to a team. Although baseball is not mentioned explicitly you can draw the conclusion that the Mudville Nine is a baseball team.
Incorrect Answers:
- **A.** There are angry spectators in the poem, but they are not the Mudville Nine.
- **C.** There is no mention of town leaders in the poem.
- **D.** The Mudville Nine is a baseball team of adults, not children.

23. Correct Answer: C *(Making Deductions)*
The poem refers to "5,000 throats," and "10,000 eyes." You can deduce that there are 5,000 spectators watching the game.
Incorrect Answers:
- **A.** There are 10,000 eyes, so there are only 5,000 people. Each person has two eyes.
- **B.** The poem implies how many people are watching.
- **D.** There are nine players on the team, not nine people watching the game.

24. Correct Answer: C *(Interpreting Poetry, Character Traits)* **I**
Based on Casey's behavior as he goes up to bat, it is inferred that he is very confident.
Incorrect Answer:
- **A.** Casey does not behave like a person who is intimidated.
- **B.** Casey does not behave like a person who is terrified.
- **D.** Casey does not behave like a person who is nervous.

Explanations for Test A Answers (cont.)

Casey at the Bat (pages 26–29) (cont.)

25. Correct Answer: C (Interpreting Poetry, Figurative Language)
Hyperbole is a form of exaggerated speech. The spectators don't want to literally kill the umpire; they are just very angry about the call he made.
Incorrect Answers:
A. A *simile* compares two things using the word *like* or *as*.
B. *Onomatopoeia* is a word that sounds like the thing it describes.
D. An *allusion* is a reference to something.

26. Correct Answer: D (Interpreting Poetry, Figurative Language, Image)
The poet describes the baseball as a leather-covered sphere to conjure up a vivid image for the reader.
Incorrect Answers:
A. The leather-covered sphere is not a bat.
B. The leather-covered sphere is not the umpire.
C. The leather-covered sphere is not Flynn.

27. Correct Answer: A (Interpreting Poetry, Genre)
"Casey at the Bat" is a ballad; a poem of many stanzas or verses that tells a story, usually of an event.
Incorrect Answers:
B. A *sonnet* is a 14-line poem that follows a very strict rhyming scheme.
C. A *cinquain* is a five-line stanza or poem.
D. A *limerick* is a five-line poem that is usually very silly or nonsensical.

28. Correct Answer: C (Interpreting Poetry)
The home team, the Mudville Nine, lost the game so the townspeople are not happy.
Incorrect Answers:
A. It was not raining during the game.
B. Casey struck out. He did not get injured.
D. Some spectators do leave the stadium, but that is not why there is no joy in Mudville.

29. Correct Answer: A (Interpreting Poetry) E
The poem explicitly states that Cooney, Barrows, Flynn, and Blake all came up to bat before Casey.
Incorrect Answers:
B. Four batters were up before Casey, not 2.
C. Four batters were up before Casey, not 6.
D. Four batters were up before Casey, not 5.

30. Correct Answer: C (Interpreting Poetry, Point of View)
The person telling the story is watching the game and seems to sympathize with the spectators as he is able to describe their feelings so well.
Incorrect Answers:
A. The umpire is involved in the event, but he is not telling the details of it.
B. Casey is the main character in the event, but he is not telling the story.
D. The spectator telling this tale does not mention the name of the opposing team or the names of any of the players. If he did, that would be a clue that he was more sympathetic to the opposing team.

WALNUT HILL LINE Train Schedule (pages 30–33)

31. Correct Answer: D (Locating Details)
The Walnut Hill station is the farthest from Center City.
Incorrect Answers:
A. Suburban Station is not as far as Walnut Hill.
B. North Madison is not as far as Walnut Hill.
C. Seven Sisters is not as far as Walnut Hill.

32. Correct Answer: A (Locating Details)
The second schedule explicitly shows that the 4:34 from North Madison will get you to Seven Sisters at 4:48.
Incorrect Answers:
B. 4:37 is the time you would arrive at Queen Lane.
C. 4:34 is the time the train gets to North Madison, not Seven Sisters.
D. 4:35 is the time you would leave Seven Sisters to get to North Madison on the other schedule.

33. Correct Answer: B (Making Deductions) E
In the General Information section it states, "If no time appears, the train does not make a stop at the station."
Incorrect Answers:
A. It's possible that the printers made a mistake, but the blank boxes are explained in the General Information section.
C. There is nothing to suggest that the blank spaces mean that the train makes unscheduled stops.
D. There is nothing to suggest that the blank spaces mean that passengers can get *off* but not *on* a train.

34. Correct Answer: A (Making Inferences)
You can infer that the ride is 29 minutes long by counting how many minutes elapse between 1:59 and 2:28.
Incorrect Answers:
B. 30 minutes is one minute longer than it really takes.
C. This is illogical. If it depends on how fast the train is moving, there could be no schedule to begin with.
D. This answer is about 2 hours too long.

35. Correct Answer: C (Making Inferences) I
While all of these options could be true, the one that is the most logical is option C. Typically, when a public area calls for quiet, it means no talking.
Incorrect Answers:
A. A soundproof car would mean that sounds from inside of the train would not be audible to the outside world.
B. It doesn't make much sense to have only a single car on the train that makes very little noise.
D. If an area calls for quiet, it usually means that talking is prohibited.

36. Correct Answer: A (Locating Details)
The schedule states that an **F** means that the train won't stop unless a passenger wants to get off or on the train.
Incorrect Answers:
B. There is nothing to indicate that the train might leave ahead of schedule.
C. This option makes no sense. A train would not be scheduled to be late on purpose.
D. There is nothing to indicate that an **F** means that there is no Quiet Ride Car.

37. Correct Answer: B (Locating Details)
The 11:02 is traveling in the direction of Center City so the next stop is clearly Summit.
Incorrect Answers:
A. Allen Lane comes before Carpenter Station.
C. Walnut Hill is where the train originates.
D. Center City is the ultimate destination of the train.

Explanations for Test A Answers *(cont.)*

WALNUT HILL LINE Train Schedule *(pages 30–33)* *(cont.)*

38. Correct Answer: C *(Locating Details)*
President's Day is not listed as a major holiday on the schedule.
Incorrect Answers:
A. New Year's Day is a major holiday on the schedule.
B. Memorial Day is a major holiday on the schedule.
D. Thanksgiving Day is a major holiday on the schedule.

39. Correct Answer: D *(Locating Details)* **E**
In the General Information section, the schedule states that the Quiet Ride car is the first car on the train.
Incorrect Answers:
A. The Quiet Ride Car is not the last car on the train.
B. The Quiet Ride Car is not the middle car on the train.
C. The Quiet Ride Car is not the third car on the train.

40. Correct Answer: D *(Making Inferences)* **I**
You can infer that one train takes longer than the other because it has to make a stop the other train does not have to make.
Incorrect Answers:
A. Traffic is not typically an issue for trains.
B. Trains typically travel at consistent speeds regardless of who the conductor is.
C. This is unlikely, as it is clear that there are occasions where trains do not stop at certain stations.

The Gift of the Magi *(pages 34–39)*

41. Correct Answer: C *(Making Inferences, Setting)* **I**
You can infer that that the story takes place about 100 years ago because the rent on the apartment is only 8 dollars, and the people in the story do have electricity as an electric buzzer is mentioned.
Incorrect Answers:
A. If the story were set in the present day, the rent would be a lot more than it is in the story.
B. You can assume that in the future rent would be much more than it is in the story.
D. There was no electricity 200 years ago and the story mentions the existence of an electric buzzer that is broken.

42. Correct Answer: B *(Recalling Details)*
The story refers to James as being Della's husband.
Incorrect Answers:
A. Della and Jim are not brother and sister.
C. Della and Jim are not father and daughter.
D. Della and Jim are not mother and son.

43. Correct Answer: D *(Plot Elements, Conflict)*
The problem is that Della and Jim are poor and Della wants to buy Jim a Christmas present.
Incorrect Answers:
A. There is no suggestion that Della and Jim can't afford the rent.
B. The doorbell is broken, but that is not the primary conflict in the story.
C. The story mentions the harsh weather and the fact that Jim needs a new coat, but that is not the main problem in the story.

44. Correct Answer: C *(Author's Style, Narration)*
The narrator in the story is not a character in the story. Additionally, the narrator can tell the reader the thoughts and feelings of Della, but only describes the actions and behaviors of Jim.
Incorrect Answers:
A. A first person narrator would be a character in the story, for

example if Della or Jim were telling the story.
B. A third person omniscient narrator would be able to tell the reader about the thoughts and feelings of all of the characters, not just one of them.
D. The second person is rarely used in the telling of fiction.

45. Correct Answer: B *(Interpreting Fiction, Character Analysis)* **I**
Della feels embarrassed and ashamed, and the reader sees that she is crying and is told it is because she is poor. This implies that most likely, Della feels frustration at having no money and sad about the fact that she can't buy Jim a Christmas gift.
Incorrect Answers:
A. Della's behavior is not consistent with a person who is joyful and patient.
C. There is no evidence to suggest that Della is angry. She is sad but it is because she is poor. Typically, depression is not connected to something external.
D. Della is sad, but there is no evidence to show that she is envious.

46. Correct Answer: B *(Interpreting Fiction, Character Analysis)* **I**
It is inferred that she is upset about losing her hair because just before she cries she is admiring her long flowing hair.
Incorrect Answers:
A. Della is sad because she is poor, but this question refers specifically to the behavior described in paragraph 6.
C. Della is not worried about Jim; she wants to buy him a gift.
D. Della is sad because she can't afford a watch chain for Jim, but this question refers specifically to the behavior described in paragraph 6.

47. Correct Answer: C *(Recalling Details)* **E**
The story states explicitly that Della is paid 20 dollars for her hair.
Incorrect Answers:
A. Della is not paid 21 dollars. This is the amount she pays for the chain.
B. At the beginning of the story, Della has $ 1.87 to buy Jim a Christmas present.
D. Della is not paid 35 dollars.

48. Correct Answer: D *(Determining Meaning, Context Clues)*
The combs are described as something that Della worshipped.
Incorrect Answers:
A. *Coveted* is not a synonym for *beautiful*.
B. *Coveted* does not mean *expensive*.
C. *Coveted* does not mean *rare*.

49. Correct Answer: A *(Interpreting Fiction, Theme)*
Both Jim and Della give up, or sacrifice, their prized possessions so they can get enough money to buy each other something the other one wants.
Incorrect Answers:
B. Duty is not what motivates Jim and Della. It is love.
C. Jim and Della are poor, but poverty is not the theme of the story.
D. Neither Jim nor Della are angry or envious.

50. Correct Answer: A *(Literary Devices, Irony)*
Irony often involves the element of surprise. The ending of this story does contain a surprise.
Incorrect Answers:
B. The futility of their sacrifice is not an example of irony.
C. The reality that they are still poor is not an example of irony.
D. The speed at which Della's hair will grow back is not an example of irony.

Test B Answer Key

1. C	6. B	11. C	16. D	21. A	26. A	31. A	36. C	41. A	46. A
2. D	7. D	12. B	17. C	22. C	27. A	32. C	37. A	42. C	47. D
3 B	8. A	13. B	18. B	23. B	28. D	33. C	38. D	43. D	48. B
4. D	9. C	14. A	19. D	24. D	29. D	34. D	39. D	44. B	49. D
5. A	10. D	15. A	20. C	25. A	30. C	35. A	40. B	45. D	50. A

Explanations for Test B Answers

The Night Sky (pages 40–44)

1. **Correct Answer: C** *(Summarizing)*
   The magnitude of stars and their temperature are the focus of the passage.
   Incorrect Answers:
   A. This statement from the introductory paragraph contains the summary of what the passage is about. The question was specifically about the section entitled "Types of Stars."
   B. The author refers to objects in the night sky, but this does not summarize the entire passage.
   D. Moon myths are discussed, but the passage is about much more than that.

2. **Correct Answer: D** *(Making Deductions)*
   An earthworm is large enough and close enough to be able to be seen without the use of a telescope or microscope.
   Incorrect Answers:
   A. A virus is microscopic.
   B. Dust mites are microscopic.
   C. Neptune is too far away.

3. **Correct Answer: B** *(Making Deductions)*
   The absolute magnitude of the sun is 4.8. A star with an absolute magnitude less than that would not shine as brightly.
   Incorrect Answers:
   A. A star's absolute magnitude would have to be greater than 4.8 to shine brighter than the sun.
   C. A star's absolute magnitude would have to be exactly 4.8 to have equal brightness to the sun.
   D. The passage explains how to evaluate absolute magnitude.

4. **Correct Answer: D** *(Recalling Details)*
   The passage explains that O B A F G K M is a classification of the temperature of stars.
   Incorrect Answers:
   A. O B A F G K M is not a classification for absolute magnitude.
   B. O B A F G K M has nothing to do with the phases of the moon.
   C. O B A F G K M has nothing to do with the distance of stars from Earth.

5. **Correct Answer: A** *(Interpreting Graphic Features, Chart)* E
   The chart clearly shows that a K-class star would glow orange to red.
   Incorrect Answers:
   B. A G-class star might glow yellow.
   C. An A-or F-class star might glow blue.
   D. The chart states that only an F-class star glows blue to white.

6. **Correct Answer: B** *(Interpreting Graphic Features, Chart)*
   The chart shows that both a first and last quarter moon would appear as half moons in the sky.
   Incorrect Answers:
   A. The first and last quarter moon would not appear full.
   C. The waxing and waning gibbous moons appear crescent-shaped, not the first and last quarter moons.
   D. The new moon is not visible in the night sky.

7. **Correct Answer: D** *(Recalling Details)* E
   The passage states explicitly that it is the sun that causes the phases of the moon.
   Incorrect Answers:
   A. The rotation of the moon itself does not cause its phases.
   B. The distance of the moon to Earth does not cause its phases.
   C. The brightness of the sun does not cause its phases.

8. **Correct Answer: A** *(Text Structure, Headings, and Subheadings)*
   The passage organizes the material in headings and subheadings.
   Incorrect Answers:
   B. Cause and effect is not the text structure.
   C. The passage does not include an index or a glossary.
   D. There are paragraphs, but all nonfiction text is organized into paragraphs. This is not the most specific answer.

9. **Correct Answer: C** *(Making Inferences)* I
   The passage tells us that the moon is the subject of much myth. Myths usually grow around things that are mysterious. Our moon is a mystery to most people, as most people have never traveled there. Myths are often celebrated in folktales and songs.
   Incorrect Answers:
   A. Many words do rhyme with *moon*, but this is not the reason there are songs and folklore about it.
   B. Very few people have been to the moon.
   D. The moon is relatively close, but its proximity is not the reason there are folktales and songs about it.

10. **Correct Answer: D** *(Locating Details)*
    The passage states that comets are made of ice and meteoroids are made of rock.
    Incorrect Answers:
    A. Comets and meteoroids are both rare.
    B. A comet does not make a streak called a meteor, a meteoroid does.
    C. This is the opposite of what is true; comets are made of ice, meteoroids are made of rock.

Explanations for Test B Answers *(cont.)*

Galileo: Father of Modern Science
(pages 45–49)

11. **Correct Answer: C** *(Making Deductions)* **I**
    The passage states that the Renaissance is also called the Age of Enlightenment. You can deduce that the era preceding it was without light (i.e. dark) hence, The Dark Ages.
    Incorrect Answers:
    A. There is no inference about reason in the passage.
    B. There is nothing in the passages that speaks to or implies industrialization.
    D. There is no such thing as The Royal Age.

12. **Correct Answer: B** *(Making Inferences)*
    Ground zero means the place where something was ignited or happened first. The passage says that the Renaissance was born in Florence and refers to it as ground zero.
    Incorrect Answers:
    A. There were no terrorist attacks in Florence during the Renaissance.
    C. Ground zero does not refer to being the geographic center of the Italian peninsula.
    D. Ground zero does not refer to how many great scientists were born in Florence.

13. **Correct Answer: B** *(Locating Details)* **E**
    The passage explicitly states that Galileo's first telescope had a magnification of 3x and his second had a magnification of 30x.
    Incorrect Answers:
    A. Both telescopes worked.
    C. The first one was less powerful than the second.
    D. The first one had a magnification of 3x.

14. **Correct Answer: A** *(Determining Meaning, Context Clues)*
    The word *spyglass* is used in the paragraph that describes Galileo's observations with telescopes.
    Incorrect Answers:
    B. You may be able to watch people through a spyglass, but that is not its meaning in this context. Galileo is watching the night sky.
    C. Spyglass is not the nickname of Galileo's first telescope.
    D. Glass is an important part of what a telescope is made from, but spyglass is not a reference to the material alone.

15. **Correct Answer: A** *(Locating Details)* **E**
    The passage explicitly states that Europa is one of Jupiter's moons.
    Incorrect Answers:
    B. Europe is a continent, not Europa.
    C. Europa is not a sunspot.
    D. The name of the school at which Galileo taught is not mentioned in the passage.

16. **Correct Answer: D** *(Locating Details)*
    The passage states that the phases of Venus help prove a theory about the position of the sun in our solar system.
    Incorrect Answers:
    A. It was already known that Earth was not the only planet in the solar system.
    B. This is not what the phases of Venus helped to prove.
    C. It did not prove how accurate Galileo's telescope was.

17. **Correct Answer: C** *(Recalling Details)*
    The church believed that Earth was at the center of the solar system and that everything else revolved around it.
    Incorrect Answers:
    A. Galileo believed that the sun was at the center of the solar system.
    B. No one thought the moon was at the center of the solar system.
    D. No one thought the sun orbited the moon.

18. **Correct Answer: B** *(Recalling Details, Cause and Effect)*
    Galileo believed that the sun, and not Earth, was at the center of the solar system. This is what caused him to be placed under house arrest.
    Incorrect Answers:
    A. Galileo did not believe that Earth was at the center of the solar system.
    C. The discovery of Jupiter's moons was not the cause of Galileo being put under house arrest.
    D. The discovery of the phases of Venus was not the cause of Galileo being put under house arrest.

19. **Correct Answer: D** *(Locating Details)*
    Galileo died in 1642, which is in the 17th century.
    Incorrect Answers:
    A. Galileo did not die in the 16th century.
    B. Galileo did not die in the 15th century.
    C. Galileo did not die in the 18th century.

20. **Correct Answer: C** *(Making Inferences)* **I**
    Galileo believed and proved certain things about the solar system that the majority of people alive in his day did not believe. He thought things in his own time, which in future times would be proved true and accepted without a doubt.
    Incorrect Answers:
    A. Living a long life has nothing to do with being ahead of one's time.
    B. Galileo did make discoveries that would be important in the future, but this is not what the phrase means.
    D. Many people invent new technologies, but it doesn't mean that they are ahead of their time.

Homework or No Homework?: That Is the Question!
(pages 50–53)

21. **Correct Answer: A** *(Recalling Details)*
    The controversy is about how important homework is.
    Incorrect Answers:
    B. There is no controversy about the importance of school.
    C. School lunches are not discussed in this passage.
    D. Research suggests that students spend too much time doing homework.

22. **Correct Answer: C** *(Locating Details)*
    Keeping kids busy is one of the traditional reasons that homework was assigned.
    Incorrect Answers:
    A. There is no evidence that homework increases test scores.
    B. There is no evidence that homework makes kids smarter.
    D. This is an illogical statement; homework is not valued because it is not done in Japan or Denmark.

23. **Correct Answer: B** *(Identifying Parts of Speech, Subject and Predicate)*
    The subject is *high-test scoring students*; the predicate is *do not do homework*.

Explanations for Test B Answers *(cont.)*

Homework or No Homework?: That Is the Question!
(pages 50–53) (cont.)

23. **Incorrect Answers:**
    - A. *High* is an adjective, *students* is a noun.
    - C. *Japan* and *Denmark* are proper nouns, *do not do*, is a simple predicate.
    - D. *Countries* is a noun, *do not* is a verb and an adverb

24. **Correct Answer: D** *(Recalling Details, Cause and Effect)*
    The author discusses new research that is changing how educators think about homework.
    Incorrect Answers:
    - A. The perspective of students is not offered in this passage.
    - B. The feelings of parents are not discussed in this passage.
    - C. Low test scores are mentioned but not as the singular cause of the changing attitude about homework.

25. **Correct Answer: A** *(Locating Details)* E
    The passage explicitly states that the average elementary school student spends 78 minutes per evening on homework.
    Incorrect Answers:
    - B. The passage says that 60 to 90 minutes of homework per evening does not increase test scores.
    - C. First grade students should spend 10 minutes per night on homework.
    - D. Second grade students should spend 20 minutes per night on homework.

26. **Correct Answer: A** *(Recalling Details)*
    The passage states that 10 minutes of homework per grade level should be done four nights per week. Second grade equals 10 + 10 = 20 minutes of homework.
    Incorrect Answers:
    - B. The passage suggests no homework on Friday.
    - C. 10 minutes of homework is the amount of homework a first grader should do.
    - D. 78 minutes is the average amount of time that is currently spent on homework.

27. **Correct Answer: A** *(Recalling Details)*
    The passage states that 10 minutes of homework per grade should be done four nights per week. Sixth grade equals 10 x 6 = 60 minutes of homework.
    Incorrect Answers:
    - B. 90 minutes of homework is not advised.
    - C. Second graders would do 20 minutes of homework.
    - D. 15 minutes is not advised.

28. **Correct Answer: D** *(Locating Details)*
    The passage states that there is a connection between the amount of time a student spends doing homework and the amount of time they are engaged in physical activity.
    Incorrect Answers:
    - A. The passage does not discuss overeating.
    - B. The passage does not discuss school suspensions.
    - C. The passage does not discuss bullying.

29. **Correct Answer: D** *(Author's Style, Persuasive Techniques)* I
    The author cites research to persuade the reader.
    Incorrect Answers:
    - A. Bullet points are an organizational feature, not a persuasive technique.
    - B. The author does not state her opinion, but it is implied.
    - C. The author does not state that she is opposed to less homework.

30. **Correct Answer: C** *(Making Deductions)*
    The passage states that homework can help a student practice a skill. Adding and subtracting fractions is a skill, so you can deduce that this would be an appropriate assignment.
    Incorrect Answers:
    - A. A research paper would take longer than the recommended amount of time a student should spend on homework.
    - B. Exercise is not mentioned as an appropriate assignment.
    - D. 90 minutes is not a recommended amount of time to spend on homework.

The Last Leaf *(pages 54–57)*

31. **Correct Answer: A** *(Interpreting Poetry, Character Analysis)*
    The main character in the poem is the last leaf on a tree.
    Incorrect Answers:
    - B. There is a bird in the poem, but it is not the main character.
    - C. Trees are mentioned but are not the main character in the poem.
    - D. The sea is mentioned but it is not the main character in the poem.

32. **Correct Answer: C** *(Interpreting Poetry, Character Analysis)*
    The reader can infer from what the leaf thinks and feels that he is sad and fearful.
    Incorrect Answers:
    - A. The leaf does not behave in a joyful or happy way.
    - B. The leaf is sad, but he is not courageous, so this option is wrong.
    - D. The leaf does not behave as if he is confused or vain.

33. **Correct Answer: C** *(Interpreting Poetry, Character Analysis)*
    The leaf trembles and clings to the branch. He fears falling into the sea.
    Incorrect Answers:
    - A. The leaf does not fear birds.
    - B. Squirrels are not mentioned in the poem.
    - D. Wind is not mentioned in the poem.

34. **Correct Answer: D** *(Interpreting Poetry, Literary Devices)*
    The leaf has the attributes of a person, so the device is personification.
    Incorrect Answers:
    - A. There are no examples of onomatopoeia in the poem.
    - B. There are no similes in the poem.
    - C. There are no examples of irony in the poem.

35. **Correct Answer: A** *(Interpreting Poetry, Imagery)*
    "Dewy, moist, and green" is a description of the leaf at the height of the glory of his youth.
    Incorrect Answers:
    - B. The old leaf is described as brown, dry, and brittle.
    - C. The poem does not describe how the bird looks.
    - D. The sea is described as being slate colored.

36. **Correct Answer: C** *(Interpreting Poetry)*
    He reminds the leaf that he is currently alone, but that if he lets go he will be with all of the leaves that have fallen before him.
    Incorrect Answers:
    - A. Old age is not discussed by the bird.
    - B. The pointlessness of holding on is not talked about by the bird.
    - D. There is no discussion about nest building.

Explanations for Test B Answers *(cont.)*

The Last Leaf *(pages 54–57)* *(cont.)*

37. Correct Answer: A *(Determining Meaning, Context Clues)* **I**
The leaf becomes unmoored when the winter roars and shakes the branches of the tree, so you can determine that the leaf gets detached from the tree and falls.
Incorrect Answers:
B. The leaf does not cling to the tree.
C. He does not meet other leaves when he is initially unmoored.
D. The leaf is not sleeping on the branch.

38. Correct Answer: D *(Interpreting Poetry, Recalling Details)*
Both the sky and the sea are described as being the color of slate.
Incorrect Answers:
A. The leaf fears the sea, but not the sky.
B. The poem does not discuss the size of the sky or the sea.
C. There is nothing in the poem to suggest that the sea and the sky represent loneliness.

39. Correct Answer: D *(Figurative Language, Allusion)*
The leaves in the sea are described as being in a school, which is an allusion to what groups of fish in the ocean are called.
Incorrect Answers:
A. A metaphor is a comparison of things.
B. A pun is a play on words.
C. An epigram is a short, funny statement.

40. Correct Answer: B *(Interpreting Poetry, Theme)* **E**
The leaf is afraid of letting go because he fears the sea. Once he changes his mind and thinks of the sea as a place where he will be joined with his friends, he is able to let go of the branch.
Incorrect Answers:
A. The leaf is entering a new stage of his life, but this is not the theme of the poem.
C. Suffering is not the theme of the poem.
D. The leaf is lonely, but this is not the theme of the poem.

Cat and Mouse in Partnership *(pages 58–62)*

41. Correct Answer: A *(Making Deductions)* **I**
Cats eat mice, and mice know this. By using flattery, the cat can have his way with the mouse.
Incorrect Answers:
B. The cat does not love the mouse. He is setting her up for the kill.
C. The mouse is not stubborn but is very compliant.
D. It is only in the cat's best interest to live with the mouse. The mouse gains nothing from this arrangement.

42. Correct Answer: C *(Drawing Conclusions)*
People would be less likely to steal something from a church because they may fear that God is watching them.
Incorrect Answers:
A. There are no better hiding places in churches than in other places.
B. Many people could go into a church.
D. Churches are not necessarily dark.

43. Correct Answer: D *(Recalling Details)*
The cat says that members of his family are having kittens and he must attend their baptisms, as he is a good uncle.
Incorrect Answers:
A. The cat doesn't say it is only natural that he goes outside to hunt.
B. There is no mention of the cat having a sick mother.
C. The cat does not say he has to go to work.

44. Correct Answer: B *(Literary Devices, Sarcasm)*
The names Top-Off, Half-Off, and All-Gone are references to the vanishing supply of fat, so he is being sarcastic.
Incorrect Answers:
A. The names are not humorous to the mouse.
C. Sarcastic is a more detailed description of the names than mean.
D. The names are definitely not pretty.

45. Correct Answer: D *(Literary Devices, Personification)*
The fact that the animals can talk is an example of personification.
Incorrect Answers:
A. Alliteration is when the beginning sound of a group of words is the same.
B. Denotation is the literal meaning of a word.
C. Hyperbole is a form of exaggeration.

46. Correct Answer: A *(Character Analysis)*
The mouse believes everything the cat says, and all the cat does is tell lies.
Incorrect Answers:
B. The mouse does not lie to the cat.
C. The mouse believes the cat's lies.
D. The mouse is not tricking the cat. The mouse is being tricked.

47. Correct Answer: D *(Recalling Details)*
The cat says, "That is because you don't go out during the daytime, and your feverish mousy mind turns to the world of phantoms and make-believe." This is another way of saying that the mouse is imagining things.
Incorrect Answers:
A. The cat does not say that the mouse has a big belly.
B. The cat does not accuse the mouse of having a secret stash of fat.
C. The cat does not accuse the mouse of having his favorite toy.

48. Correct Answer: B *(Literary Devices, Foreshadowing)*
The cat will soon make the mouse all gone by eating her.
Incorrect Answers:
A. The fat is all gone, but the name does not foreshadow that.
C. The mouse does not eat the cat.
D. It does not foreshadow the end of the story.

49. Correct Answer: D *(Interpreting Fiction, Restatement)*
"You see, that is the way of the world," describes the fact that cats and mice are natural born enemies. They are predator and prey.
Incorrect Answers:
A. Mice do not torment cats, they fear them.
B. "The world is a dangerous place" is not the best restatement of the last line of the story.
C. The last line of the story is not about trust.

50. Correct Answer: A *(Literary Devices, Irony)*
Irony usually contains an element of surprise. It turns out that the cat and the mouse are not in a partnership at all. The mouse's partner winds up eating her.
Incorrect Answers:
B. There is nothing ironic about the fact that cats and mice are mammals.
C. The fact that animals don't talk is not ironic.
D. The fact that animals don't live in houses is not ironic.

Test C Answer Key

1. D	6. A	11. B	16. C	21. D	26. C	31. C	36. B	41. B	46. D
2. B	7. C	12. C	17. B	22. B	27. A	32. B	37. C	42. B	47. B
3. D	8. B	13. B	18. B	23. B	28. D	33. D	38. D	43. D	48. C
4. D	9. D	14. A	19. A	24. C	29. A	34. C	39. A	44. C	49. A
5. A	10. A	15. D	20. D	25. A	30. D	35. A	40. C	45. B	50. C

Explanations for Test C Answers
How Silk Is Made (pages 63-66)

1. **Correct Answer: D** (Locating Details)
The passage states that the *Bombyx mori* is the name of the silkworm.
Incorrect Answers:
A. Silk moth is not the official name of the silkworm.
B. Chinese moth is not the official name of the silkworm.
C. *Bombyx* is not the official name of the silkworm.

2. **Correct Answer: B** (Locating Details)
The silkworm is flightless, so this is false.
Incorrect Answers:
A. It is true that the silkworm is blind.
C. It is true that the silkworm eats mulberry leaves.
D. It is true that the silkworm spins a cocoon.

3. **Correct Answer: D** (Determining Meaning, Definition)
The passage states that a cocoon is also called a chrysalis.
Incorrect Answers:
A. The larva is also called the caterpillar.
B. The egg is not called a chrysalis.
C. The filament is not called a chrysalis.

4. **Correct Answer: D** (Locating Details)
Sericulture is the cultivation of silkworms to produce silk.
Incorrect Answers:
A. Sericulture is not another name for the *Bombyx mori*.
B. Sericulture is not the ancient name for the Silk Road.
C. Sericulture is not a type of fabric.

5. **Correct Answer: A** (Determining Meaning, Restatement)
The passages talks about metamorphosis in the context of a process of development.
Incorrect Answers:
B. Metamorphosis does not mean cocoon spinning.
C. Metamorphosis does not mean the unwinding of a filament.
D. Metamorphosis does not mean hatching eggs.

6. **Correct Answer: A** (Interpreting Graphic Features—Flowchart)
Step one says that a silk moth lays about 300 eggs at a time.
Incorrect Answers:
B. It takes 25 days for the caterpillars to gain weight.
C. It takes 2,500 cocoons to make a single pound of silk.
D. Caterpillars get 10,000 times heavier by eating mulberry leaves.

7. **Correct Answer: C** (Interpreting Graphic Features—Flowchart)
Step 13 is winding the filament onto a spool.

Incorrect Answers:
A. This is Step 10.
B. This is Step 7.
D. This is Step 3.

8. **Correct Answer: B** (Interpreting Graphic Features—Flowchart)
Step 11 describes the killing of the pupa.
Incorrect Answers:
A. Step 10 details cocoon storage.
C. Step 1 details the egg laying.
D. The last step (14) tells how many filaments are needed to make a thread of silk.

9. **Correct Answer: D** (Interpreting Graphic Features—Flowchart)
Steps 4, 9, and 11 require 25, 3, and 8 days respectively, so you can estimate that you would need a minimum of 36 days to complete the process.
Correct Answers:
A. It takes 25 days just to fatten up the worms.
B. It takes 8 days just to dry out of the cocoons.
C. It takes 3 days just for the caterpillar to pupate.

10. **Correct Answer: A** (Making Deductions)
The Chinese could make a product that everybody else wanted, but nobody knew how to make. You can deduce that this would make them rich, and riches would have made them powerful.
Incorrect Answers:
B. Having something that others want usually does not create weakness, but the opposite.
C. Silk production would not have created famines.
D. The very fact that they were the only ones who knew how to make silk had a big effect on the growth of their civilization.

Thanking the Animals (pages 67-70)

11. **Correct Answer: B** (Locating Details)
The passage clearly states that taming is a part of domesticating animals.
Incorrect Answers:
A. Pets are domesticated, but that is not how domestication is defined.
C. Tool making is one way in which bones were used, but it does not define domestication.
D. Animals are used in medical research, but this alone does not define domestication.

12. **Correct Answer: C** (Recalling Details)
Livestock are animals that are used for food. Sheep is lamb, which people eat.

Explanations for Test C Answers *(cont.)*

Thanking the Animals *(pages 67-70)* *(cont.)*
Incorrect Answers:
- **A.** Americans typically don't eat tigers.
- **B.** Americans typically don't eat mules.
- **D.** Americans typically don't eat dogs.

13. Correct Answer: B *(Making Inferences)*
The passage clearly states that animals are used to help meet basic needs. Since entertainment is not a basic need, you can infer that a bear performing in the circus would not be considered helpful in this context.
Incorrect Answers:
- **A.** A dog sniffing for a bomb helps to protect people and keep them safe.
- **C.** Sheepherding helps to meet the basic need of food and clothing.
- **D.** The wool that sheep provide helps to make clothing.

14. Correct Answer: A *(Making Deductions)*
An animal that eats many different types of food has a flexible diet.
Incorrect Answers:
- **B.** An animal that can only eat one thing does not have a flexible diet. It actually has the opposite.
- **C.** An animal that eats only meat has a rigid diet. It can only eat one thing.
- **D.** An animal that only eats worms does not have a flexible diet.

15. Correct Answer: D *(Locating Details)*
The passage explicitly states that some animals don't breed while captive as they dislike enclosures or cages.
Incorrect Answers:
- **A.** Resentment is a human feeling. Animals can feel fear and stress.
- **B.** Aggression is given as a reason for not domesticating an animal, not for why they will not breed in captivity.
- **C.** A flexible diet is not the reason an animal won't breed in captivity.

16. Correct Answer: C *(Making Inferences)*
An animal that reaches adulthood quickly is ideal for domestication. Eleven months is the least amount of time presented in the options.
Incorrect Answers:
- **A.** 18 months is not the shortest amount of time offered.
- **B.** 20 months is the longest amount of time offered.
- **D.** 12 months is not the shortest amount of time offered.

17. Correct Answer: B *(Interpreting Graphic Feature)*
The timeline is read from left to right, so the dog was domesticated first.
Incorrect Answers:
- **A.** The horse was domesticated next to last.
- **C.** The honeybee was domesticated last.
- **D.** The cow was not domesticated first.

18. Correct Answer: B *(Making Deductions)*
The latest date on the timeline is 3500 BCE. An animal domesticated after that would to the right of the honeybee.
Incorrect Answers:
- **A.** If you put it earlier than the sheep, it would indicate that it was domesticated earlier than the sheep.
- **C.** If you put it before the cat, it would indicate that it was domesticated earlier than the cat.
- **D.** If you put it between the cow and the cat, it would indicate that it was domesticated much earlier than it was.

19. Correct Answer: A *(Distinguishing Fact from Opinion)*
The author's statement summarizes the facts provided in the passage.
Incorrect Answers:
- **B.** The author does not state his or her personal opinion but one might infer that the subject of animals is of interest.
- **C.** The author does not share his or her personal feelings about animals in the passage.
- **D.** Pets are part of the discussion, but domesticated animals are important for many other reasons as well.

20. Correct Answer: D *(Author's, Point of View, Making Inferences)*
The author has titled the piece "Thanking the Animals." Typically, people say thank you when they want to acknowledge what another has given.
Incorrect Answer:
- **A.** There is nothing in the passage to imply that the author has a greedy attitude toward domesticated animals.
- **B.** The author respects the contribution of the animals, but that is not the same as kindness.
- **C.** There is nothing in the passage to indicate that the author resents the animals.

A Woman's Right to Vote *(pages 71-73)*
21. Correct Answer: D *(Recalling Details)*
The passage states in the first paragraph that suffrage is the right to both vote and run for elected office.
Incorrect Answers:
- **A.** The right to vote is only a part of suffrage.
- **B.** The right to run for elected office is only a part of suffrage.
- **C.** The right to equal pay was mentioned in the passage, but it is not a part of suffrage.

22. Correct Answer: B *(Recalling Details)*
The first sentence of the passage states that 18 is the age you must be in order to vote.
Incorrect Answers:
- **A.** Twenty-one is not the correct answer.
- **C.** Twenty-five is not the correct answer.
- **D.** Sixteen is not the correct answer.

23. Correct Answer: B *(Making Inferences)*
The passage states that the suffrage movement began in the 19th century. The 1800s is another way to describe the 19th century.
Incorrect Answers:
- **A.** The 1900s would describe the 20th century.
- **C.** 1920 is the year in which the 19th amendment was ratified.
- **D.** The passage does not mention the year 1776.

24. Correct Answer: C *(Locating Details)*
The passage states that an important women's conference was held in 1848 in Seneca Falls, New York.
Incorrect Answers:
- **A.** Seneca Falls is not the site of the first Civil War battle.
- **B.** The birthplace of Elizabeth Cady Stanton is not mentioned in the passage.
- **D.** The 19th amendment wasn't ratified in Seneca Falls, New York.

25. Correct Answer: A *(Making Deductions)*
Not allowing a child to drive a car is a safety consideration and not an example of discrimination. Discrimination implies that an able individual or a group of individuals is not allowed to do something on the basis of race, gender, or religion.

Explanations for Test C Answers *(cont.)*

A Woman's Right to Vote *(pages 71–73)* *(cont.)*

25. Incorrect Answers:
- **B.** A person being prevented from doing something on the basis of race is an example of discrimination.
- **C.** A person being prevented from doing something on the basis of gender is an example of discrimination.
- **D.** Option A, B, and C would all have to be incorrect for this option to be correct.

26. Correct Answer: C *(Recalling Details)*
The passage says that the Women's Rights Movement suspended their activities during the Civil War to help focus on freeing slaves.
Incorrect Answers:
- **A.** The Women's Rights Movement was not made illegal.
- **B.** Women did not stop caring about the right to vote, but they felt that freeing the slaves was a more immediate need.
- **D.** Protesting for the right to vote was not considered rude during the Civil War.

27. Correct Answer: A *(Locating Details)*
The passage states in paragraph five that NAWSA means National American Woman's Suffrage Association.
Incorrect Answers:
- **B.** There is no National Association of Woman's Suffrage of America.
- **C.** There is no National American Women's Movement.
- **D.** There is no National Women's Suffrage Movement.

28. Correct Answer: D *(Locating Details)*
The passage states in the fifth paragraph that the 19th amendment guaranteed women the right to vote.
Incorrect Answers:
- **A.** The 20th amendment deals with the beginning and ending dates of the presidency and vice presidency.
- **B.** The 15th amendment guarantees the right to vote regardless of race.
- **C.** The 21st amendment repeals prohibition.

29. Correct Answer: A *(Locating Details)*
The passage states that the 19th amendment, granting women the right to vote, was ratified or passed into law in 1920.
Incorrect Answers:
- **B.** The women's conference in Seneca Falls, New York was held in 1848.
- **C.** The passage refers to the 1890s but not the year 1890.
- **D.** The year 1800 is not mentioned in the passage.

30. Correct Answer: D *(Locating Details)*
The last paragraph in the passage states that in 2012, there were about 100 women serving in the United States Congress.
Incorrect Answers:
- **A.** In 2012, there were six women serving as governors.
- **B.** The passage state that 66% of the people who voted in 2008 were women.
- **C.** This is not the correct answer.

Equal Pay for Equal Work *(pages 74–77)*

31. Correct Answer: C *(Identifying Main Idea)*
The main idea in the first paragraph is summarized in the sentence: "One area in which women have had a long struggle is in the workplace."
Incorrect Answers:
- **A.** The first paragraph implies that women have suffered from discrimination, but this is not the main idea.
- **B.** There is no mention of workplace rules in the first paragraph.
- **D.** The suffragettes are mentioned in the first paragraph, but this is not the main idea.

32. Correct Answer: B *(Identifying Cause and Effect)*
The second paragraph explains that men going to fight in WWII caused women to take up their vacated jobs.
Incorrect Answers:
- **A.** World War I is not mentioned in the passage.
- **C.** Suffrage is the right to vote and run for office.
- **D.** The Lilly Ledbetter Fair Pay Act did not cause women to enter the workforce.

33. Correct Answer: D *(Determining Meaning, Context Clues)*
Paragraph four discusses how the Equal Pay Act made it illegal to pay women less than men for doing the same job.
Incorrect Answers:
- **A.** High and low paying jobs are not discussed in this passage.
- **B.** The salaries in factories and offices are not discussed in this passage.
- **C.** The term *income gap* does not mean the same thing as the Lilly Ledbetter Act.

34. Correct Answer: C *(Locating Details)*
President Kennedy signed the Equal Pay Act into law.
Incorrect Answers:
- **A.** President Obama signed the Lilly Ledbetter Fair Pay Act into law.
- **B.** President Bush is not mentioned in this passage.
- **D.** President Clinton is not mentioned in this passage.

35. Correct Answer: A *(Identifying Cause and Effect)*
The passage states that Lilly Ledbetter sued Goodyear because she was being paid less for doing the same work as the men.
Incorrect Answers:
- **B.** Ledbetter was not forced to work longer hours than men.
- **C.** Men were paid more not less than she was.
- **D.** Lilly Ledbetter chose to retire. She was not forced.

36. Correct Answer: B *(Recalling Details)*
The court argued that Lilly Ledbetter should have filed a complaint within 180 days of receiving her first unfair paycheck.
Incorrect Answers:
- **A.** There was proof of sex discrimination; the court said Ledbetter waited too long to report it.
- **C.** The court argued the opposite of this.
- **D.** Ledbetter's work performance was not a part of the suit.

37. Correct Answer: C *(Recalling Details)*
Because salary information is usually kept private, Ledbetter had no idea that she was being paid less than her male coworkers.
Incorrect Answers:
- **A.** Lilly Ledbetter did not put it off. She didn't know it was happening.
- **B.** The passage does not mention anything about a conversation between Ledbetter and Goodyear.
- **D.** Lilly Ledbetter had legal representation.

38. Correct Answer: D *(Locating Details)*
The Lilly Ledbetter Fair Pay Act allows a person to file a complaint of wage discrimination within 180 days of their most recent paycheck.
Incorrect Answers:
- **A.** This is not what the Lilly Ledbetter Fair Pay Act states.
- **B.** The length of time you have been employed at a company is not a part of the Ledbetter Act.
- **C.** This is not true. You must file a complaint within 180 days of your most recent paycheck.

Explanations for Test C Answers *(cont.)*

Equal Pay for Equal Work *(pages 74–77)* *(cont.)*

39. Correct Answer: A *(Locating Details)*
President Obama signed the act in 2009.
Incorrect Answers:
B. The Equal Pay Act was signed in 1963.
C. The Lilly Ledbetter Act was not signed during World War II.
D. The Lilly Ledbetter Act was not signed in 2012.

40. Correct Answer: C *(Making Inferences)*
Daughters are female, and the Lilly Ledbetter Act helps people address wage discrimination, which is usually suffered by females.
Incorrect Answers:
A. You can assume that the President does love his daughters, but this is probably not why he mentioned them.
B. It is very unlikely that the President thinks of Lilly Ledbetter as his daughter.
D. The President's daughters were very young in 2009, so it is unlikely that they supported the Lilly Ledbetter Act.

Say Cheese *(pages 78–82)*

41. Correct Answer: B *(Identifying Main Character)*
Keyshawn is the main character and the narrator of the story. All of the events in the story revolve around Keyshawn.
Incorrect Answers:
A. Mr. Folietti is a secondary character in the story.
C. Mary Anne runs the coffee shop, but she is not a main character in the story.
D. Mr. Lee is Keyshawn's teacher, but he is not a main character in the story.

42. Correct Answer: B *(Making Deductions)*
Because the name of the shop is a play on words, it will probably be more memorable to customers.
Incorrect Answers:
A. Having the product in the name is helpful, but it wouldn't necessarily make it the best choice here.
C. The name of the shop is short, but a short store name is not always the best store name.
D. Ease of spelling might be part of a good store name, but it is not the only thing involved.

43. Correct Answer: D *(Recalling Details)*
Keyshawn says that his favorite cheese is Parmesan, and this kind of cheese is from Italy.
Incorrect Answers:
A. The story mentions Blue Wensleydale from England, but this is not Keyshawn's favorite cheese.
B. The story mentions Camembert from France, but this is not Keyshawn's favorite cheese.
C. The story mentions Bundz from Poland, but this is not Keyshawn's favorite cheese.

44. Correct Answer: C *(Recalling Details)*
The story states that Foli's father purchased the store from the fishmonger, whose name was Cohen.
Incorrect Answers:
A. Foli did not purchase the building from Cohen.
B. Mission Millinery did not purchase the building from Cohen. It was probably the other way around.
D. There is no candlestick maker in the story.

45. Correct Answer: B *(Making Inferences)*
Keyshawn is looking through lots of old photographs of his community, and it is making him feel as if he is going back in time.
Incorrect Answers
A. There is no mention about Keyshawn watching a movie about time travel.
C. There is no room in the library that is called the time machine.
D. Keyshawn is not really in a time machine.

46. Correct Answer: D *(Locating Details)*
Keyshawn observes that as the photos get older and older, the streets get more primitive—from paved, to cobblestone, to simply dirt roads.
Incorrect Answers
A. The newest road would be paved.
B. The roads before the paved ones would have been made of cobblestones.
C. There is no mention of the roads being bumpy.

47. Correct Answer: B *(Recalling Details)*
Through his internet research, Keyshawn discovers that a *millinery is a place that sells ladies hats. A milliner* must be the person who designs and makes ladies' hats.
Incorrect Answers:
A. A *fishmonger* sells fish, not hats.
C. A *greengrocer* sells fruits and vegetables.
D. A *cobbler* fixes shoes. There is no mention of cobblers in the story.

48. Correct Answer: C *(Making Inferences)*
You can infer that Foli hangs the photos in his store to show respect for all of the hardworking people who have owned the shop before him. Foli's respect for the past is also evidenced by the fact that he kept the painting of the fish, from the days of the fishmonger, on the wall in his cheese shop.
Incorrect Answers
A. There is nothing in the story to infer that Foli's actions regarding Keyshawn have anything to do with business skills.
B. Photos are decorations, but this is not why he takes up the project with Keyshawn.
D. You can never select *all of the options* unless all of the other options are correct.

49. Correct Answer: A *(Recalling Details)*
Keyshawn gets the idea to take a picture of himself and Foli when they are hanging the older photos in the shop.
Incorrect Answers:
B. It is Foli's idea for Keyshawn to do research about the past.
C. There is no conversation in the story about Keyshawn being open-minded about cheese.
D. Keyshawn does not have a plan to become a milliner.

50. Correct Answer: C *(Making Deductions)*
In the final section, the story is taking place in the present, while the characters hang photos of the past and ponder what the store will be in the future.
Incorrect Answers:
A. Researching the past was done in a previous section of the story.
B. No one is researching the future in this section of the story.
D. This answer is not logical.

59570085R00057

Made in the USA
Middletown, DE
12 August 2019